LOVE DISTINGUISHED - SERIES ONE

LOVE

Books

By Agene Justice Onotiemoria

1. *Love*
2. *The Wonderland of Love*
3. *The Heart of Love*
4. *Sweet Bitter Love*
5. *Stolen Love*

LOVE DISTINGUISHED - SERIES ONE

LOVE

AGENE JUSTICE ONOTIEMORIA

BOOK 1 OF A 5 BOOK SERIES
Love Distinguished

1. Love

2. *The Wonderland of Love*

3. *The Heart of Love*

4. *Sweet Bitter Love*

5. *Stolen Love*

BOOK TITLE: **Love**
Book Series, Love Distinguished 1 of 5

WRITTEN BY AGENE JUSTICE ONOTIEMORIA
Paperback ISBN: 978-1-909132-28-3
eBook ISBN: 978-1-909132-29-0

Published By:
APMI Publications
In Partnership with Truth for the Journey Books
Email: publications@alanpateman.com
www.AlanPatemanMinistries.com

Acknowledgements:
Cover Design Copyright APMI
Senior Editor/Publisher: Dr. Alan Pateman
Editing/Proofreading/Research: Dr. Jennifer Pateman
Computer Administration/Office Manager: Dr. Dorothea Struhlik
Cover Image Credit: www.PosterMyWall.com

Unless otherwise indicated, all scriptural quotations are from the King James Version of the bible.

*Where scriptures appear with special emphasis (**in bold,** italic or <u>underlined</u>) we have edited them ourselves in order to bring focused attention within the context of this subject being taught.*

Dedication

I dedicate this book to my unquestionable God, who saw me as a worthy fountain pen to reach the world. I dedicate it to my biological brothers and sisters, both at home and abroad, including my parents who always keep up with their support, you are my backbone. In addition my mentors and benefactors, well done, let's work together as a team for solid achievement. I also dedicate this work to all of my well-wishers, pastors, brethren and friends, whether home or abroad your "Hi," means a lot to me. Keep it up. God bless you all.

Table of Contents

Acknowledgement

When I got this idea from God, I really did not know where to start; until His Excellency—Almighty God used my co-worker (Yaw) who triggered my morale to pen down the great idea God deposited in my skull for the people. I appreciate him for that. I thank my pastor Dr. P. J. Bassey of Christ Faith Assemblies Castelfranco Emilia (MO) who proof read most of my manuscripts. My thanks also goes to pastor Osei of Pilgrim Christian Ministries of Reggio Emilia, my mentor.

My thanks goes to brother Norbert who did the computer setting. My thanks goes also to my colleague: my son—Lucas who also did part of the computing. My thanks goes to my second cousin, Mr. Prince Frances Ebhohimen Udin who initiated the typing. My thanks goes to my younger sister Joy Agene who did part of the typing. My thanks goes also to master Sylvester Ehijiawmusoe my friend, a brother and a mentor (kudos). My thanks goes to all my family members, home and abroad. My mum and my dad: Mr. and Mrs. Agene Jeremiah Ogun for their direct and indirect support; thanks sir and ma. God blesses you all.

Foreword

There is no best summary or equation to help us define true love. If there was, then grammarians should be able to tell us the simple meaning of this four letter word LOVE. On a mere human scale of things, love is deceitful, mysterious and cheating. Whereas true love takes the Spirit of the living God to practice it, for Jehovah God Himself is Love (1 John 4:8). God simply knew how it was going to be with mankind in the act of practising love towards one another, which is why He gave Himself the name, LOVE.

It takes the true love of God for the world to be peaceful and it is the summary of the Ten Commandments of God. Really, if you look at the whole thing, (with a true love for your neighbour), you can't hurt them, but dwell in peace and harmony.

Introduction

Humanly, we all discuss love as though it were an easy job. We mentioned the conditions to make up a true relationship for love. We speak of heaven and earth with our various mother tongues, to portray the character called LOVE. The practical aspect will tell you how it is with you. You don't need a story, neither do you need a prophet to tell you what you are expecting in your life, when you are already inside the whole system.

Honestly, love is too broaden and heavy. If love were an object, nobody could carry it due to its weight! If it were a house, eyes can't just behold the whole thing at a time. If it were a company, the population of the global community couldn't meet up with its required labour force. If it were a book, till death, no one can finish studying it. If you say that love is a million, you haven't started to count and your calculations might be wrong.

Therefore, we could simply say that the activities of mankind would determine the type of love we can all agree exists in the world. In other words, your dealings and mine towards each other birth the types of love we could boldly claim that exist. No statistic can tell. If any fellow says, "I love you," you are not wrong by taking a twice glance at him.

Of course, that signifies something unspeakable from the onset. Imagine at first sight one just starts to love what one doesn't even know so well! There are colours inside of colours. Something could appear red to your naked eye, whereby it is truly black. What do you do? You are to watch it for sometime in order to master its originality, else you might make a mistake of a wrong choice.

CHAPTER 1

Love Defined

Love the Expression of Passion

Love is the result of interest developed over any fellow individual, animal or even inanimate object, at first sight and deeply felt. It is a whisper from the depth of the heart, which embraces every part of the body system. It is an admiration one has or shows over nature or the artificial. Love can as well be defined as an expression of passion, whether good, bad, direct or indirect, sincere or cunning, right or wrong, as the case may appeal to the one concerned. And love is a gift from God, which one can exercise both visibly and invisibly.

The believers were commanded according to the scriptures to love their Creator with all their might and heart, including all that they had (Matt. 22:37). Thus, whichever way love springs up in you and you express or exercise it, it is simply love but it must correspond to sight and be felt from a genuine background with the right motive. Love changes as the mind changes.

The School of Love

Coming to the crux of the matter in the school of love, I emphatically stress from a human perspective that there is no love among the human race. It's unarguable. If you have eyes, you can definitely tell what you see. If you have feelings, you can as well tell how you feel over situations around you; whether or not they are pleasant to your human visibility and feelings or not. After all, sight and feelings in most cases can even dictate a reaction for you. You just can't tell me that happiness can still instantaneously be in your mind after being hurt. It is not possible.

Are you not a human being? You can't tell me that you will be so happy the moment you stand to your feet after a stumble where you fell so very badly. I believe your container can never be so instantaneously full of joy! For example, you cannot humanly be yourself when on return from work, the only family house you have was ablaze and you were left with relatively nothing.

Spirit and Flesh always Contend with Each Other

You can't tell me that when you're conscious of being ridiculed by a certain group of people, you're suddenly full of confidence and joy! Except God has helped to mutilate the flesh, which reacts to that which is in your human nature, you just can't overcome it's rival. This means, spirit and flesh always contend with each other. In most cases, if you are prepared in advance, hardly can you fall victim.

Rolling and dealing with an ocean of dilemma, who on earth can still maintain a complete heuristic approach? Except the flesh had been dealt with a long long time ago, would you have overlooked such a mockery? Otherwise it must manifest itself to react to your hurt.

Contrary to our Expectation

Sometimes we do experience things that are contrary to our expectations from our neighbours, (eventually every one of our dealings with our fellow humans!) A date can even give us unexpected attitudes, which could result in the action of agape. In every circle, if we all are informed, we must know that whom we are going to meet, may not satisfy us exactly as we would want. We just have to be prepared to be tolerant in the whole circle, otherwise, there will always be quarrels.

At times, you will be the one to retire quarrelling with a fool, who cannot meet up with a standard. It will even come to a time that you will be the one to caution yourself saying: *"I can't continue to quarrel every now and then because they just can't do above their standard, in order to impress me or meet up with my prerequisites."* We can only practice likeness, if at all ideal likeness towards one another.

Before I proceed, I must not hesitate to carefully tailor my words to substantiate my opinion in this regard; in order to make my beloved audience know some types of love. And more also, the perspective from which this issue is coming from and as well as where it is going, must be strictly maintained even appraised. Otherwise, to the ignorant, the work of paradox is an action with foolishness. Humanly, we don't know it all. The average individual lacks the knowledge to determine how easy and how far life deals with a person.

Chapter 2

Agape Love

The Manifestations of Expression

Love is a vital requirement by all races and even animals. There comes a time in a person's life that he or she may need a hug, just to feel human. And that is why even some animals need petting; mostly dogs and cats or other domestic animals. For example, some partners just can't sleep without the other. Others instead, can't eat alone. Natural reactions and manifestations are entirely different from one individual to another.

Categorically, love can come by surprise. For example, when one doesn't work for it, yet is suddenly being showered! It is selflessly a love exercised by one, upon another, without any expectation of a return payment or fleshly gratification.

A popular adage says: *"One should learn to mind reactions even before dining and winning with people."* Dining and wining with those who have no love for you is uncalled for.

No matter the circumstances one faces, the challenges of life are bearable. Remember, you are not the first to go through that terrible situation. It is such that is commonly happening to every man (1 Cor. 10:13).

The Workshop of Love

May be there is a lesson the Lord God wants you to learn for your maturity. There are workshops or lessons about life, which the Lord God Himself permits, in order for us to learn about our individual lives and whereby the Holy Spirit is our personal teacher (Isa. 30:20-21). He will still provide us with the power, comfort, strength, courage, wisdom, knowledge and belief, even the escape root if necessary (including the faith), to finally surpass the whole challenge.

There are so many histories of exemplary people that experienced and surpassed theirs. And so, your case is not an exception. No single element that does not like a conducive atmosphere. As for me, I prefer dwelling with desirable people, who desire me for good as friends, (whether of lower, middle or higher class). At a particular point in time, who would not want my case, down to the bottom of his or her belly!

Due to the quality of agape love, people with the gift do exercise unchangeable passion over their neighbours. The percentage is of equity between whoever may be concerned. Considerably, there is a genuine dealing among the circular operators. In this love, if your level of dealing does not match with your required level by your recipient, meet up with your standard to aid him or her up.

You are aided by a God who sent a genuine messiah in order to be able to administer what you are errand to the concerned. God is aware of our secret dealings towards one another. He knows those that care and those that do not care. And so, He—God will never allow the givers to lack, otherwise, the ministry of generosity will close. He actually makes sure that He goes round to sponsor it, in order to encourage the ministers. May the good Lord resource someone in order to be able to finance their project, in Jesus' name.

Agape Love is Exercised Unconditionally

This is the type of love, which is unconditionally exercised. God is the master practice of this love. We actually saw it when God Almighty demonstrated it to humanity through atonement, which demonstrated the ministry of reconciliation by His Lordship over mankind. In that scenario, Jesus purchased the hostages from Satan, for His kingdom of light, by salvation (Acts 17:11).

Such a redemptive action remains indelible in the history of mankind, the beneficiaries of the Almighty God, through Jesus Christ our Lord. It is a gift anyway. You cannot really offer what you don't have. Those who are deeply rooted in this type of love are truly crazing, even with the intention to die for someone who is rightfully in the position to benefit from the exercise.

Whenever a problem is presented to them, and peradventure delay sets in due to a time factor, they are no longer themselves until they've fulfilled the ministerial assignment, by providing a solution. This is the more reason you hear someone tell the other, *"I will die for you."* It is not as if the operator in question is a fool. Capitally NO; (and if you reason it that way then you've got it all wrong). It's just that he or she can't, because the fire inside of him is too much for the job or action. Some people who try to make research on this type of love, end up giving it names like, *craving* and so forth.

Agape is No Ordinary Love

You see, really, let's comes to the truth of the whole matter. Good is never fully exercised or practised effectively and efficiently until theory and practice are a balanced equation. For example, if you are a good person, fine; but prove it and let's see it in action, with a true love from the heart. We aren't just talking about ordinary love here, are we?

We simply mean a situation whereby a fellow with all voluntary readiness, will go the extra mile with another, without considering any payment or feeling any sense of superiority. He or she is not discouraged from helping you. Relationships between people with this type of love, from any class, does not count on age before any help can be rendered.

Agape: Exercises No Tribalism

Agape love doesn't take any offence to heart. In other words, he or she is never forced to forgive, before even pouring out mercy on whoever is concerned. It is totally a pity that everybody is growing and not yet matured in this type of love. And wrong advisers can't beat it, because it knows where to pass. It understands even your feelings before conclusion is made over a rapport. It has no tribalism in the exercise.

Agape love has no time to associate with a bunch of fools against one another. The major target is to ensure that justice and love prevails. In addition, agape doesn't gossip about anybody. Also, the little it can do, it does and then leaves the rest to God.

In the secular world, some elements are fed with negative info. For example, your parents are a witch and wizard. Since they have no personal means to get the fact cleared, they take on to that. The reaction that follows is to abandon their responsibility over them. Imagine! The little life that is not fair in the first place is made miserable with poor parents.

What a tragic attitude with some elements! Tomorrow, when they are gone, you see the wicked children in the best of attire, with beads on their necks and hands, with a claim to be celebrating the burial of parents they never cared for! Agape love for example, (regardless of negatives) will say that they were the best of parents, (for simply bringing them into the world). And that until such parents are no more, they will make sure they are well taken care of, even with the little they can afford.

Similarly, due to what some are brain-washed, they look at their siblings as animals, even worthy to be renounced and denied of brotherhood. Oh, thanks be to God Almighty that the act of ritualism is not possible with hostility. It would have been too rampant!

Agape doesn't do all that. Cohabiting is with all harmony. In companies, no one turns a stumbling block to each other, in regards to promotions and a fixed contract. Minding of one's business, without force, is one of the attitudes.

Agape: The Peacemaker

Agape will never resent, nor yield to any act of disturbance. Agape love can never laugh at you. It doesn't condemn, humiliate, insult or even assault. It does not cause any embarrassment to anybody. It does not gloat on a victim of circumstances. It can only correct you of your errors and omissions, politely with the spirit of love.

It is a peace maker. It is sincere and honest. It treats and judges fairly. It is selfless and considerate. It embraces to uplift the good spirit or soul, which was downed. It carries others along without even complaining. It treats everyone equally. Her government is quiet with good governance. And her dealing is equity.

I am not going to go to work until you are done with the problem of health, which you find so very difficult to explain to the doctor. Am I understood? I guess I can sense how you feel. For example, *"You cannot go to that hospital all alone, while I just sit back and watch you toil in all of it alone. And I promise myself never to abandon you to pass the whole stress alone. I am going to make sure you are okay."* These are the characteristics of agape love. No download for outside inspection for your let down.

There are people who are schooled and some are still schooling with scholarship, (such benefits do not come from their same blood, in most cases). These charities do not consider having estate in the entire world before aiding their beneficiaries. A giver never lacks. Moreover, blessed is the hand that gives, than the one that takes. If you are favoured you are favoured.

Agape uses Good Samaritans

After all, many who were humanly regarded as paupers, ended up owning their own homes that were built for them by some good Samaritans. These were people who never dreamt of having personal roofs over their heads, only to be blessed with them. It is actually amazing when the gifted, are exercising their gifts on the dues, and that doesn't make evil men gain advantage over us. It pleases God mostly when they are blessing those that are truly in need.

If my audience can permit me, I will put it on us that that which you have does not belong only to you, rather it is for you and for those God gave you to take good care of. You are fulfilling your assignment or your ministry when you begin to help them.

Jesus fed the 4,000 and then the 5,000, who were present with Him in the presence of God, just to hear the good news. He had pity on them for they came all the way from their respective residential places, in order to listen to the message of salvation and the end of the age.

Agape: Freely Expressed & Given

Agape is when you are fed unconditionally. And thus, if someone actually clothe you up, feed you, hospitalise you, employ you, establish you in order to get you something doing, buy you a car, treat you of your ailment, buy you drugs or medicine, sponsor your career without any demand in cash or in kind from you, he or she has actually exercised agape love over you.

I have personally seen where aged people took free good care of children (and others unrelated), as babysitters. This is common with white and black in the western world. It is out of a true love.

I want to equivocally say a big thank you to all genuine men of the living God who take the problems of others as their own, by turning towards fasting and prayer, until it's resolved by God. What love! Jesus said: "No one has greater love than to lay down his own life for his friends" (John 15:13).

Please, clap for the true men of God, even though it is their ministerial work assigned to them by God. Not everybody can fulfil appointment; that's one thing you should know. It is not humanly easy. The power of service comes from God. Not everybody can actually feature his or her neighbour's case in search for a solution. May God bless them for their selflessness.

The Politics of Agape

Politically speaking, one example of agape love is evidenced when the UN takes care of a less privileged nation in times of war, starvation, tremor, earthquake, volcano, flood and other natural disasters. This is rendered voluntarily without expecting any payback as appreciation. Similarly, in the same vein, some kind-hearted farmers render voluntary assistance to other farmers who need a helping hand to meet up with their farming system.

You and I know that farming is a lucrative business. Besides the benefits, it is very tedious a job to do for a living. It is the mother of employment in every nation. Statistics declared that farming owns 25% of the labour force or employment in any nation in the world. Imagine, most people claim farming to be a hard job, yet one would do it freely for another. Such benevolence is truly commendable.

Also, some personalities have voluntarily sponsored some candidates by campaigning for their political careers, without asking for any return payment. Barack Obama got this benefit from some Americans in January 20, 2009 when he became the president of America at the age of 49yrs (born August 4, 1961 in Honolulu, Hawaii, United States).

Additionally, some individuals have rendered such humanitarian aid as: free lighting, portable waters, good roads, maternity homes, orphanage facilities, even destitute buildings of town halls, electricity, just to mention a few. Some have gone as far as providing these benefits (on behalf of the government) for the welfare of others, which is an act of unconditional love. If agape love sees a situation of dire need, it doesn't laugh it off, rather it looks for a way to provide a solution, for the Lord's glory.

Agape: Sowing Seeds of Divine Favour

I have personally witnessed this in the changed atmosphere of those receiving favour and blessing from others, as a divine seed of agape dropped by God Himself, right into their midst. This is done for the express purpose of His glory.

As the song goes, *"What goes around, comes right back around."* Why am I saying this? Because God can use anything to bless you. He will prove that everything He has created is useful to Him and by Him. Can I hear somebody say, *"Thou shall not underrate anybody"* in Jesus' name.

I hereby put it on somebody to ruminate, in order to know where they have rendered help to anybody in the past, and whether they have exercised this kind of love or not. Inside all of us, not excluding myself, there is agape love as a gift, yet if we don't exercise it (on the right people with good motive), we've got it all wrong.

Agape: More than Transactional Eye-Service

For instance, the law of dividend is respected in agape. But there are certain individuals who'd never do anything, unless they cheat on you in the transaction. And generally speaking people do tend to rate your background, (but it's not so in this regard), before you are given your due treatment.

"To err is human, to forgive is divine." Agape forgiveness is one hundred over a hundred percent and simply over looks side-talk, not even remembering to mention it in the prospect. And regardless of what is being offered in return

(or reciprocated), the love being offered is the same, because agape is much more than mere eye-service.

CHAPTER 3

Eros Love

Intoxicating Passion & Desire

This love is romantic and erotically passionate with all sexual desire. This is the kind of love, in which the younger generations are mostly intoxicated. For example, at times you hear individuals say a variation of the following sentiments:

"I love you baby. Ever since I set my eyes on you, I haven't been myself. And life had not been the same in the sense, your love waves me like west wind is to trees of Lebanon.

I am trying to carefully arrange what I have to tell you as not to get you offended. Your personality matters to me because I don't even know how you may take it. But I strongly believe that 'no mouth dreads the expression of a strong matter'. So, what is worth being said, is worth being said. Without beating around the bush, I am in love with you!

Wooing the Opposite Sex

There must be something special about you and it is beyond my explanation; I must confess and it is yet to be all figured out so very clearly. I am perplexed. I just can't let you go unless you are mine. Please, do not turn down my proposal; for I love you dearly and I actually do not know how to say it in such away that will not hurt your feelings.

Please, permit me to use that statement just to be able to express my feelings. I am too heavy with much to express on the inside about being in love with you. And I don't mind being a fool to you. I love you to cut the whole story short. You are the only sugar in my tea. You know I just can't do without you, as cloth over nakedness. You know I love you more than my mum. What else could an impeccable girl like you need from a guy like me?

Look, I am available at your disposal. I don't mind surrounding you like a bullet-proof vest. I am a guy who doesn't want any flies to peach on your skin baby. Could you be my queen and I be your king. Baby, if you ask me to die I will die for you. I am in love with you and without you I am short of appetite.

Woman makes a man. I can't do without you. Do you get me? I just want to spoil you with my cash if you allow me. My hand bag, I am droning in love with you. I promise to serve your family till I die. It means yours is secure, without being impulsive. I promise if you even at all accept me, I will buy you the best ride – car of your choice. My only comprehensive text one. My latest foam.

What would you have me do by saying, 'Wow!' with surprise to my promises?

Do you think it is a fake? Do you view my expressions as impossibilities? And that I am saying it to have you as just a figure head? Never, that can't be. Do you know what? I must take extra good care of this golden body of yours. If only you accept my proposal, I promise you will over enjoy me. You will never regret your deed. I promise I will take extra good care of you, I repeat.

"Your Love is Driving Me Crazy!"

Do you know something? I am going to give you one million names. And I mean every word of my comment. My lexicon one. My mirror, my only love. Could you be my Juliet and I be your Romeo? My fountain pen one. I could talk till tomorrow without being tired just to prove to you how much I am in love with you. I am stupid and foolish to your love, baby can't you see? I just can't control myself anymore because of you please, I love you. And your love is driving me crazy!

My heart is not only beating, pumping and pushing you a whole lot of love, but also whispering to me a small gentle cool voice like the nightingale saying: 'Where on earth did this angel come from?' Baby you were indeed lucky to have been endowed with this extra beauty of yours, like no other. If only I can have this epitome around me, I will be okay the rest of my life. I have never all my life set eyes on this beautiful face. Wow.

Please, can I have your conversation? If I don't marry you I will die. I doubt it if you know how it is with me right now. Angel please, take me to meet your parents right away. I am desperately in love and I just can't hide my feelings. I can't wait to have you as my only love. If anybody likes, he or she could call it madness. If it takes to be called a mad-man to have you, I am glad."

Another way that other smart guys toast is: *"Hi my name is Barry Victor nice to meet you."* As if she was expecting something from him. *"And you?" "Oh, I'm Sandra Fellow-men." "Wow! Sandra Fellow-men, what a nice name."*

Did you send her an errand? Men, you are getting down so soon. *"Please, if that be the case, can I have your number?" "What for?" "So that we can discuss it better I wanted to have a word with you. Please, I wanted to talk to you."* She answers, *"Not that I am trying to be rude or something, it's just that whenever you guys demand for a number from any single lady, you must be up to something!"*

Luring Her To Bed & Nothing More

"Baby, trust me I am different. Why not give me a try and see what I have to say." (An old adage says, 'a trial will convince you'). *"Alright, you take the number before the bus stops." "Thank you. The pleasure is mine." "Bye for now. We shall speak by phone okay?" "Yeah, I got it with all jubilations."*

Original can never flatter, no matter what. Not even a sign of trill can you sense in his attitude at his first approach to you. *"Thank you. Pleasure is mine."*

Such are some of the yearnings and toasting of many single guys; most especially those with the intention of wooing the opposite sex, with all the collective impressions it takes to achieve their aim, at all costs. Just to lure her to bed, that's all nothing more. One week of love!

The question is, does the guy in question, the toaster, really mean business? Does he really mean what he says? Only the true God can tell what is in the mind of an individual regarding a proposal for a relationship.

Look! It's not all about bombarding a lady or a single girl with so much heaven and earth about yourself, whereby you know within your mind one can discover totally nothing but lie and deceit. You cannot expect any responsible single lady, well brought up from a good home to jump along with you simply because you can fry hair on your head; with sweet tongue and seem so very romantic in your approach!

True Love is Authentic not just Romantic

The fact that you possess every artificial qualification, as expected by the lady in question, (just to conceal your reality, which is inwardly a total fake and fallacy), is not a guarantee to succeeding her, if at all. Quote me anywhere. No matter how smart you are or convinced of yourself, you must fall backward. Did I hear someone asking, *"How?"* The truth is not far fetched, in the sense that the foundation is baseless.

Guy, do you know something? In the long run, even if you succeeded in the beginning, you must backfire. Did I hear someone say, *"It's true. You can say that again"*? All is a fantasy. How can a guy, who suffers to search for a lady in the cold, sun, rain and due, conclude that he's no longer interested? Can someone groom up a true relationship for nothing? Something must be wrong somewhere.

It might be that he has already gotten what he wanted and now concludes that it's no longer useful to him anymore.

He couldn't be so bold to conclude negatively just like that, but I can put it on us that such is to be researched for a detail. There must be a mystery behind it. More than 50% of motives are for advantage, in some relationships, after which are dumped!

No Genuine Relationship Ends Disastrously

It's the same thing with some fake ladies, who are equally in this business of using guys only to dump them, forgetting the law of diminishing return. The issue about toasting in most cases depends on the point of contact; that determine as to how the toaster and the toast will demonstrate the action in question. And the language they're going to use also depends on the amount of contact.

The simple fact is that, no genuine relationship ends disastrously, I must confess. For example, an approach in a circle like: herbalist, native doctor, hospital, open market/ supermarket, school, church, bus-stop, on bus, on flight, on train, at or in the train-station, in car, on motorcycle, shops, workshops, companies, offices, farm, roads, kitchen, sitting-room, bathroom, toilet, palm plantations, rubber plantations, or coco plantation, (in short orchards are quite different). As you can see, that language tone must be different all together, no doubt.

Without Segregation

There are a series of examples in history, one of which is a case of a guy known as Jack Dawson in a film titled, Titanic. He was travelling to America and ran across Rose

DeWitt Bukater who he rescued from committing suicide. How could such a beautiful girl of her calibre get so fed up, to warrant such an attempt as suicide? As Jack rightly said, *"Life is precious."*

Jack added, *"If you won't listen, then I'll die with you!"* He spoke out of love, just to discourage her from killing herself. *"Who are you? I don't know you,"* Rose replied and insisted on continuing with her attempt. But Jack reminded her about the frozen ice! However, after all was said and done, the only appreciation that the people of Rose could show to Jack, was to invite him for the wedding ceremony party, on a different floor of the ship.

Jack felt shy and timid as he approached with his invitation, simply because he didn't have the appropriate outfit for the event. However, fortunately for Jack, a lady gave him her son's suit, just to help grace the occasion. All was for love, which does not count on people of the same cadre. They all dined and wined on the same table and exchanged conversation without segregation. Thank God for Jack, the moment of dilemma was taken care of.

Disgrace to Matrimony

Many guys have succeeded in using sweet tongues to remove many half-married women from their marriages. The matrimonial figure head's, may God have mercy and help them. Imagine a situation whereby a married woman, who has taken her husband for an umbrella where invisible men enter freely, with free entrance and free exit! (Why marriage? You are very correct to ask).

Only to discover in the long run, that it's still as though they were single, when guys used to deceive and disappoint them. *"Oh! Had I known,"* they say. Yet it's too late already, you are in the middle of the red sea. May God have mercy and forgive the fake disappointment and disgraces to a matrimony.

Extra Marital Affairs & Fake Homes

Majorities sleep with neighbours, who rent in their apartments. Some connect with married women lovers through their women friends. Some have retired from their husband's houses and become their brothers girlfriend or concubine! Some homes are fake. Some have even resigned themselves to helping their fathers. What a life! And in working places and schools are just enough for the unfaithful to make their choices of their extra marital affairs.

Why should one close their eyes and begin to dance acrobatic, when one knows they're heading no where? Again one would ask, *"Why marriage?"*

No matter how you are so bothered with all curiosities, you can never find a real contact with readiness to disclose to you nothing but the truth; never, no, never I repeat. Except you just want him to lose his customers. Someone who feels like telling the simple truth, may amount to a redundancy over his or her spiritual customers or even be faced with some quarrel. My brethren, there must be unspeakable mysteries.

Dangerous Truth & Unquenchable Light

No preacher goes straight to the point. It is a dangerous truth with unquenchable light, only those with whom the

Lord God had helped can boldly speak it without fear. It takes the Spirit of God, with sound mind and boldness to speak the original truth.

You can say it when you have killed the flesh and are fully delivered, in that you no longer go there. You can only say it, when you take your mind off the benefits and enrichment that the flesh offers. No longer fascinated with all the intimidations of wealth from the negative side, from which God doesn't receive any glory.

It takes the divine sacrifice of God to take your focus and mind off the pleasures and enjoyments of life, which do not embrace the praise and glory of God. But just in case the Lord God permit you by His grace, then you are freed. However, don't lure anybody (you don't know the kind of grace that covers them), else God may hold you responsible, because each destiny is different.

CHAPTER 4

Philia Love

Brotherly Love

This is also known as brotherly love. How you carry your siblings, relatives, even parents matters. I must say this is a big ministry in the sense no one comes to this earth all alone. Hence, mind you, as you treat one another, those among the same blood with you (even of the same lineage) may be accounted for to the King of nature, the Sovereignty.

It is a serious matter in the sense, you could be surprised only to be judged, based on that little thing you did to your brother, your sister, your uncle, your aunty, your father, your mother, your nice, your nephew, your in- laws, your kinsmen and women and felt it does not matter and so nor does it necessitate any act of apology and so you went away with it.

We all have responsibilities. We were born to serve one another for good (Gen. 1:28). I also thank God for Christ. The relationship between brothers and sisters in Christ can also come in here. As the called of God, there are obligations we must all fulfil as one body of Christ, hence, the brotherhood of Christ (1 Pet. 2:17) have this one gift—love to share among themselves.

Cultural Practices

The cultural practices in this context makes you hear 'A' calling 'B' thus: brother Tony, sister Grace, so on and so forth. Normally, these are people who weren't worth or merited calling none of those extra respect being attached or added to their names in the world circle. Human distinction is something else all together, you just can't know how it functions even against the supposedly respected figures of our society.

It was literarily indicated in accordance to culture of the saints, to somehow express a certain degree of closeness in relationship as a body (believers) of Christ. Now the analysis comes for somebody to know much about relationship between siblings.

Why were you given a sum to build a house for your father, mother, brother, sister, uncle, son, daughter, nephew, niece, cousin etc., and you misused the money? Why did you divert that money, which was supposed to be given to your uncle for personal use? You did that because you felt nobody would ask right?

Because none of your uncle's children are at home, the drugs you were supposed to administer to him, you sold them to make money and when his condition became critical you were still the first to complain to alert everybody to his attention. Why for goodness sake? Why did you poison your niece to death, because her pregnancy will testify what you did to her in secrete?

God Notices How you Deal

Hey, you took your brother's picture to a hired assassin, in order to help you kill him to silence the issue of him returning to ask for his money, which he actually gave you to build an estate for him? Remember how you did the whole thing.

God saw you when you were actually going about snapping pictures of the on going project of another person, with a claim to be your brother's. You did that just to conceal your trick and cheat. Is that right? You, why did you take your wife's pants for a ritual?

You want to make money overnight and then get married to another woman and start enjoying your money? Was that not your plan? Remember, nothing is hidden under the sun. The naked eyes of the true living God observes everything on a daily basis. If you like to treat your neighbour's right.

What A Post-Mortem Love!

How do we all really care for our loved ones? Is it only when they have problems, such as one is dead and you'll no longer see him or her again that you begin to render help such as buying a casket? What a post-mortem love! An idol mind is the devil's workshop they say. Your brother's son wasn't having enough money to go to school and you could not help, but now that you heard he is reported apprehended by the police you appear to bail him.

If it's only those things which yield back a positive return for you that causes you to render any assistance, then you are a devil and you need to repent. Your uncle wasn't having the money to buy the recommended attire for his coronation, which they alerted you for help, yet you did not care. Yet when he died you began to buy clothes and an expensive casket for his burial. Your person will be looking for food when he or she is alive, even when you are throwing away some remnants and you are here visiting him with flowers in the cemetery. Please, judge yourself if you are rational.

A Humanistic System

Look at you, who were never there even when you were needed most. There was a time when you changed your phone number because you never really wanted anyone getting in contact. Behold as bad things happen, your chest is number one, identifying with a claim saying, *"They are my family!"* Where are we really going with this questionable living system of yours, which is so humanistic? Somebody should please have a conscience to feel for others.

If you are a man, what can you prove to the world on the basis of leadership? And if you are a woman, what good example can you really prove to the people? Please, make impart for life is not forever. Is it by cornering your husband to your family side alone and then look for every way to poison his mind against his people? Is that why you are a woman by his side and even a life partner? Why are you so sentimental and segregative towards your fellow human being?

The Pattern Of Jesus

Use the pattern of Jesus to dwell with your people rather than looking forward into thinking that there is a free family out there. No matter how hard you may try to wash your biology completely off of you, they are still your people; that was how God ordained it. If you taste outside, you find out that home embarrassment is still far better.

Mind you, America you so claim to be paradise, no tree produces money there except you work, nothing is going to put anything in your pocket. No food on your table, if you don't do anything good to make it up.

Embrace your siblings somebody, your relatives and as many that connect to your blood-lineage as a person. There is a divine reason why you were born in their midst. No matter how you may humanly strive with family, (communal, local, state, country, or continental zone) and what have you by asylum in order to effect a natural change? It will never work and you will answer the quarrel with God. Any act of perversion must be punished.

CHAPTER 5

Casual Love

Familiar Acquaintance

This is the most common kind of love among all races. We just knew the motor. And that is the popular saying by those that practice this kind of love. For example, I know the driver of that car or of that bus. Somebody can recognise another, which is a normal thing that exists in the connections between human beings. Everybody practices this love.

In most cases, it usually does not go with sincerity or even honesty. It changes from time to time. Its flexibility determines what is on board at a particular point in time. It is to a different dimension in the sense, you could be well or ill-treated. Being familiar with many people doesn't mean that there is a cordial relationship between you. Rather it's just facial or partial recognition.

This is the reason why at times two people who seem to be very good of friends, suddenly become enemies over a mere crash. There could also be a situation whereby you just have a kind of person at least you both have some heart to heart talk. This is to relieve you of the perpetual "down" in your spirit, from the challenges you are facing in life. He or she might eventually be the type that is porous (loose in talk), before you realise it your secrete is already airborne. And that tells you that your relationship with such a one is of dissimulation. And that you got no friend.

Fake Friends

Being fast in trusting people so very closely as bosom friends could be dangerous at times and it could also be the worst a man can do to himself. Be very careful whom you trust yourself to. Evil is a destroyer. Even in the case of help, if any evil agent helps you and you are successful it is no longer a mission by the devil.

People claim some fellows as friends for a prestige or even effizy. This is done for many reasons, for example to gain respect from among personalities, also to obtain freedom or to gain in someway. There are popular means of casual friendships which take place today, through all means and device. And some do honestly make friends through social medial; Facebook for example.

A fellow could apart from the above channel of love, find a friend through pictures of a friend or a home of a relative.

Similarly, through direct or indirect contact, which may be a phone call, SMS or so forth. Making a friendship has uncountable motives behind it. It is also advisable that one should make a friend with the aim to achieve positive results for the glory of God.

The Human Ego in Relationship

How about friends at school? Are they really friends after school? The human ego of some friends usually doesn't augur well with them. For example, imagine two very good friends, that when one passes out from school before the other, such a distinction can occur between them that one begins to regard the other as an incompetent fool. No more visiting each other, as they did before!

Take a very close look at the idea of making a new friendship; you find out that there is a reason that lies in it. You can hear those who can't hide their feelings say: *"We don't belong to the same class"* Why? Because they just can't continue to pretend every time they're around you. May evil that men carry along and around you fade to their faces in Jesus' name.

Remember, when you were just coming up he or she used to have certain value by you. I am talking to you, the tool in the hand of the devil. You never saw then that he was not good enough to make a friend. I dare you to take a closer look at cloth, how it has value to nakedness. I am not saying you should follow a betrayer of trust. I am not saying you must accept a thief for a friend. I am not saying you should accept friendship with a lover of people's wives. I am not against any reaction that rebuke reasons outside normal friendship or even a relationship; please, get me right. To every action, there is a corresponding genuine reason for a reaction.

I happened to run across two opposite sexes of students. The girl gave the boy a ride by her bicycle on the front pole as they were coming from school, guess what happened, as they both exited from the school compound. I observed that the girl's breasts were indirectly romancing the boy's back. This is not usually common after school. They may not even have a word of greeting for each other after school due to the fact that the relationship may never again that very closed. Humanly, almost we all normally remember those we often see on a frequent basis.

Bullying within Families

Culture, like parental care or pets, may not permit such a level or degree of intimacy, even of any casual relationship. Some battle with restriction in the houses. Bullying from parents even to go to church is a tug of war. Do you know how many are bullied down as a restriction from going out. Somebody, you can say that again. Many are faced with members of families tortured as a measure of restriction. And whereby what we are trying to prevent are too much, only the Lord God can save issues.

We cannot blame some parents in their actions towards their children. Some histories are really sad in the sense, if you hear how some girls are being raped even impregnated, you will pity them and also blame their parents who allowed them with such a freedom. A lot of sad histories have been told about girls that lost their lives to ritual in an attempt to go out just like every other girl. To this end, some strive to ensure that they bail themselves of this shackle of public castigations by limit the movement of their children to some extent.

Keeping Bad Company is the Issue

It is not a question of going out that is the problem, the problem is the companions. If you keep bad company, there is every possibility that one day, smoke must testify that there is fire on the mountain. If you are going or moving out with a friend and his or her discussion is always obscene, please, I suggest you cut off that friendship if you can't do anything to change it; except you need embarrassment should you continue to keep that relationship.

You must do everything possible to prove your parents completely wrong over assumptions they gather in mind against you. The mind can think or reason anything. And so, don't let their assumption read or manifest positive in you. You must do everything possible to prove it completely wrong about you by them.

Carrying a bad impression towards your children due to sad histories of some youths with allurement is so very bad, please parents I beg of you. If as a child your going out is to go and learn how to steal, withdraw and stay in the house. If your going out is to gossip, I suggest you stay in the house. If you don't have anything special to do, study your books and watch television; pray and read the bible. It is better to be a home boy or girl than to be a thief or being raped (even impregnated out there), or die for ritual.

Wrong Influences

Many have been used for rituals because of wrong movement. If you are not careful with a friend, you might just be initiated into fraternity some day. May God save His people in Jesus' name. We all have had stories of people being poisoned to death by drink and food, even beheaded, and more. Stop moving by fashion. Stop going out by fashion. Stop dressing by fashion. Stop eating by fashion. Stop making up by fashion. It is a total craziness to actually live like that. Wrong fashion can birth anything disastrous.

CHAPTER 6

Sibling Lovers

Natural vs. Unnatural Love

Some people so like their brothers and sisters as if they are something else or even a pet! They chat together every time you see them. Some of them can even go the extra mile by sacrificially making every effort to support and train them up, (whether older or younger). I don't dispute any act of benevolence to that extent.

They either defend them or use them for a defence. Particularly, with the African race, even though I might not have been humanly sent, I must say a big thank you to God for Western ideas, for the less privileged. Enabling them to shoulder every responsibility that concerns an individual, to his or her family, home and abroad.

I do not mean staying back home to take up opportunity that concerns one to earn means of surviving livelihood cannot birth any assistance to one's beneficiaries. No not at all. Please, get me right. I am trying to be elicit for more understanding for your sake and good. But travelling abroad also facilitates in the helping process.

I must commend you on your generosity brother/sister. Keep it up. Some of you are indeed pilots, sailors, drivers and even more, well done. You are all indeed true messiahs. You may never know what you did and what you are truly doing, I tell you, you are all making impart, God is your strength; lay hands. Oh you are truly unbelievable. May He—God be praised. I truly believe that the Lord God is proud of somebody.

Benevolence

Benevolence is a gift and those who exercise it on the needy, must be truly rewarded. Blessed are those that provide their families with their needs. You are unbelievable. I can feel and see some of you fulfilling the ministry of Christ. He had compassion on the needy. He fed people. He healed the sick and raised the dead. He set the captives free. We saw the dumb speak. The lame stood to their feet and walked. The blind saw and the deaf heard, during His time on earth and His ministerial days.

Jesus Christ said that poor people can never be finished in the world (Deut. 15:11). That statement denotes that God uses it as a control measure of a check and balance in order to know those that care for one another and those that do not care. One can ordinarily be taking care of someone in the midst of his or her family, with the right motive in praise to God and that may be the measure of his or her judgement by God on that day.

True, the day of reckoning may be a total surprise to individual persons on how minor the issues are going to be. And he or she may be surprised to be justified and made righteous with the true living God. Behold, eternity is yours. For God said I will have mercy on whom I will have mercy (Rom. 9:15); while on the contrary, a little thing might just send someone to hell.

Be Careful How you Treat People

Be careful how you treat people. During Christ's ministry on earth, He said: "I was in prison you visited me, I was naked you clothed me, I was thirsty you gave me drink, and I was hungry you fed me." Then the disciples asked the master, "When were you going through those stresses that we never saw you?" He replied and said, "Inasmuch as you have done it to one of the least amongst you, you have done it onto Me" (Matt. 25:35-40).

The selfishness in the heart of mankind was drastically reduced to a minimum level on hearing this. Today aren't people actually generous? Those that would have suffered were no longer denied of certain benefits and opportunities because the truth is unveiled by Christ. I pray for somebody, you shall know the truth and the truth shall set you free (John 8:32).

Who would help them is made available at their disposal. It is only when a messiah fails to discharge his or her responsibility on the dues around them that the beneficiaries suffer during which you see some evil people that can't hold it, begin to gloat that life is dealing and treating the victims badly. This is why you often hear thus saying: *"When good men fail evil men succeed"*. May that not be the portion of somebody in Jesus' mighty name.

When the resources are available, the project becomes a less problem. On the contrary before now, many apprentices dropped out from their various institutions of learning (to acquire the skills and knowledge), due to an inability to meet up with the requisites for the specific allotted period of training by the authority.

People with a Giving Heart

There were naturally endowed intellects who would have changed the world for better, yet due to the lack of a sponsor, they dropped out of schools (even gave up their ideas) so the gifts eventually died within them. When a problem prolongs too much, patience can humanly die out. What a tragedy! There are people with a giving heart but because they don't have people around them, suffer the pain with them. What a collective responsibility! Due to inability to fulfil the ministry of charity, a good hearted person is sick.

Commending the effort of the people in the diaspora does not underrate the home bases. I guess I am understood? I do not mean by saying that the home bases are not also trying. The beneficiaries are very proud of having them in their midst. Due to their cooperation, they work as a team.

Expensive schools have been attended by some poor families. You can see graduates today in some homes that were not humanly regarded. We bless God who has people that He uses as tools to work miracles in the lives of others. May His name be praised.

"Abomination!"

They say that advantage has disadvantage. Secondly, some same-bloods, see each other as lovers in bed! The foolish and possessed demonic girls, feel that the only way to show appreciation to a generous brother, uncle, brother-in-law, nephew, cosine etc., is to seduce him in order to show it to him in kind.

Imagine! They actually allow evil to soil their conscience by crossing the natural border of common brotherhood, for the abominable actions thereof. They start making love to one another. Can I hear somebody say, *"Abomination!"* If an external body comes into their midst, to approach a relationship, he or she will be so very disappointed, due to the disgustful thing they will be doing to his notice. There is no scientist on earth that is so special in the act of monitoring brothers and sisters in bed relationship as lovers.

Look, a husband could ironically escort his wife to her brother's place for sex. Ignorantly, the man may actually not know. If she says they have a family meeting or a discussion, he can't just suspect her. They could even on arrival, if care is not taken, be found acting closely (with the pretension of having a private talk) not knowing that they are having their quiet moment. My brothers, God forbid us to be a party to such a kind of love.

A similar case is where you also hear that someone is proposing to a lady only to hear that his proposal is being given out for another man by her fake brother, sister or a relative (for a business), besides him, her finance.

Families within Families

When the action births evidence (pregnancy), they may succeed in terminating the baby before it escalates and disgraces their indulgence. Although such secret intelligent emitters are highly punished anyway by the natural Chief of all judges. Whatsoever a man sow shall he reap (Gal. 6:7). However there are some stubborn foetuses that just can't be spoiled, which helps disgrace them of their actions. Even so, when they're giving birth, the child resembles the actual operators.

This is why you hear people say, *"The baby is just a replica of the brother!"* Perhaps, blood is thinker than water. You see, thank God. Who told you? *"Go to details about soup, you will dislike anyone actually prepared with an undesirable fish." "It is only a pond that can tell whose water came in it."*

Many families are inside families. Jehovah God saw it first and then seriously warned Moses ahead to tell the people of Israel that there should be restrictions and certain limits on relationships amongst them (Lev. 18:6-18).

Unlawful Sexual Relations

I want to officially bring us to a little fact about immigrants. The majority of people who have been confronted with the probe over cases of this nature have relocated (by force), to other nations of the world. And if it were truly possible to relate some of these stories (to reveal some present realities), many people would be shocked.

May God deliver us in Jesus' name. I am sure the ears of the rational will tingle over it. Apart from the direct and indirect sacrifices made to subside the calamities, the shame alone is enough to drive any guilty or any convicted fellow to where he cannot easily be traced. Those who ran from home think they can actually avert the penalty of their crime. Yet of all the effort put in place by the crime agents, it cannot really cover the sin without punishment.

Every Secret Sin will be Punished

Another unseen problem with some of the global single ladies is the damaged wombs they incur from such terrible acts (as a punishment over atrocities). I tell you not all bareness is a spiritual attack from the devil. Every secret sin must be punished. The fact that God will have mercy on you doesn't mean He will completely remove the punishment, especially when you have already sown the seed (and must reap it). Pray to God so that you don't continue in the same sin.

Reaping the Consequences

Paul the apostle suffered for what he did to the people of God, even dying as a martyr. In some localities, such cannot be tolerated because the law is relatively enacted from the constitution of God and as such carries certain powers to hand over consequences as strong as bareness.

The highest intelligent ritualism in the world is the one actually organised by demonic powers, to be carried out amongst brothers and sisters, (in the field of relationship and having intercourse with one another). Believe you me that must be a crime of the highest order.

You can never believe that your date is having an affair with their same blood. No matter how smart or intelligent you may think you are, to this issue, you can't just smart it up to catch them in the act. Some are operating on higher levels (even with PhD's) by doing it with their fathers! The daughters of Lot are condemned by the preachers, yet some people are doing it till tomorrow, without seeing anything bad about it.

If you ask some ladies, who dis-virgin themselves, they just can't boldly tell you. It is because it was their father or one of their same bloods. Even if they go far a bit, it is still within the family circle, with relatives like: an uncle, nephew, cousin, or in-law etc., whomever it is within the family circle. (I do mean physical).

Love existing among siblings cannot be over emphasised. There is also another intelligent aspect where they actually serve as your mentors, while inwardly they are your den enemies that you can never think of. They are actually destroying you. They put you in a cage of limitation and give you partial comfort.

Ignorance Invites Deception

"At least I am okay, half baked is better than none," you say out of ignorance. They put you in those chains of limitation,

simply because they just don't want you to exceed their allotted level for you, so they leave you with partial peace of mind. For example, they put you on the reins with sickness, only to leave you with partial good health. Actually hiding the virus, so that you imagine all is well with you; no longer praying for good health in order to completely battle it over.

Or say your income is flowing gradually, as if it's supposed to be that way and you claim to be comfortable with that. Oh no! You must refuse to settle with anything less than normal. It's either you get it all, or not at all. So, I say fight it in prayer, until you succeed in Jesus' name.

Give God Complete Control

Intelligent powers are cheats. Once they succeed in depriving you from a portion of your blessing, they'll actively pursue the rest, so be wise (2 Cor. 2:11; Matt. 10:36).

Additionally, evil spiritual members, which fight you in your body also need to be gotten rid of. Since a human being has a spirit, a soul and a body, you protect them in the name of Jesus. Negative powers must be denied access to the chambers of our bodies. This can only be done by allowing God to have complete control over everything, to His glory (Matt. 6:33, Heb. 4:12).

Can you be wise enough to know the enemies in the house? Except God gives you spiritual eyes you can't really know who your complete enemies are within the family circle.

Only God's Spirit gives us Insight

Another thing is that you can't humanly fight, except you are charged by the anointing of God (through the help of the Holy Spirit) with spiritual insight. You can't just raise a standard against them, even if you might have close knowledge. You might even feel so very good; cherishing something inside of you, little did you know, it was actually a symbol of the enemy's deposit and you're afraid to lose pleasure if you remove it.

Number one, you are afraid to lose anyone on the basis of human amongst you. Two, you don't want to mourn any of them simply because you love them dearly. Your siblings are your first genuine friends. They are your pride. They are just like gold on your crown. It is actually good having brothers and sisters around one. It springs energy from within.

That is why some fake conscience people use them to wage war. Forgetting that when they are lost to war, it's a total loss. For example, *"My brother is in the police force. My brother is a soldier. My brother or sister is in the navy or is a customs officer etc."* They begin to look for trouble, assuming that their sibling will defend them with the authority of their uniform.

Do you know something, it is a complete mistake to forget what's inside that uniform; a life with breath! The breath could stop and when life is gone, that's the end. Such a thing is what you are recklessly joking with. It is a pity.

Trouble Makers

Powers can lay hold on some people (to embark on evil), making trouble in order to ensnare their target. If an evil kingdom is against any united family and it just can't succeed with all other mechanisms or strategies by attempt, it will introduce rash into the family or system. You can see now that you are the rash. I am ashamed of somebody.

I can sense it from one's breath right away with all solace: *"Oh! I have delivered my brother for them to kill." "Oh! I sold my sister to the enemies." "I have exposed my angel, my warrior, my king, my queen, my pride for enemies to destroy."* A similar case was what Judas Iscariot did against Jesus Christ.

Let us figure out what Judas wanted, which was to use Jesus to wage war against the Roman empire and for Christ to be king overnight. However, Judas failed to understand that Jesus had not come to rival with earthly kings over leadership position. He actually misunderstood the complete motive why Jesus was born.

As a relative, he felt, using Jesus to wage war was the ultimate solution to the oppression they were experiencing from the Roman empire. When he realised his mistake, he felt sorry and committed suicide. What an inexplicable mistake! *"O God, please forgive me."* But, *"it's too late to cry when the head is actually off,"* they say.

It is true that God may forgive you. But your sibling will never come back, even if you cry till tomorrow. You allowed human pride to overwhelm you and deliver your siblings to the menace, which sent them to an early grave. These were the very people who would have sponsored you in those universities and taken you places in the world. Yet they were offered up so easily to heartless diabolical people for destruction. May God help you.

Protect your Blessings

Can someone now see why one must protect what he has? I am ashamed of some of us, who are tools for a rash in families, against those who would have been useful, not only to the family but also to society in general.

Therefore, I emphatically stress that one must protect what one has. The truth of the matter is, everything is important and useful. I hereby dare you to, *"tame your soup for an evening meal."* In other words, *"maintain your rag to linger long, in order to cover your nakedness."* And, *"don't destroy your tent so that you can't find a place to lay your head."* The question is, if you destroy your MC who will introduce you?

Just as, *"a few words are enough for the wise,"* one can easily tell who his or her siblings are. If they are your clothes protect them, otherwise you'll go naked. If he or she is your soup, conserve and preserve them, or else you'll die of hunger. If he or she is actually your tent, protect them or be prepared to die in the cold. (I could be your personal prophet right now, in this analysis of the human phenomenon). Take to it and be wise.

Mistaken Identity & Misplaced Intimacy

Hello, you and I know that too much of everything is bad. So then you, husband to your wife and father to your children, why are you not always seen around your family? Your younger brother now seems the biological father to your children and the true husband to your wife (except in bed), why?

You know what human beings conclude, in the context that any responsible single girl (who always sees your brother with your children) wouldn't want to ask (as not to be laughed at or tagged a husband seeker). The nature is that a good thing is reared.

There could be things that your brother does not know about marriage, which he might mistakenly end up introducing or inculcating the spirit of a wrong culture in your children. Once children grasp any character or knowledge contrary to the societal conformity, it is taken already by them and there is little or nothing anybody can do about it. Except by God's grace and His total intervention through deliverance, they won't be set free.

Same thing with your wife. Too much degree of intimacy or closeness could birth adultery between a fake brother in-law and a heartless sister in-law who respects not the culture of matrimony.

Do you know that there are level of domestic assistance your younger brother would be rendering to your wife on your behalf and on account of that, she would want to show appreciation in kind if care is not taken. Don't you rather think by occupying your brother with your family and some of your supposed active responsibilities you may be denying him of his family in time?

Shifting Responsibilities

Shifting of responsibility like that every time is not right and you can be responsible for his being delayed. You know that accountability exists in every destiny. Let's deal with one another fairly for God's sake.

I have seen many young single ladies becoming indirect baby-sitters for their sisters. It is very hard for any single good guy to come in closer (to find out whether she is the biological mother of those children or not), as she is always catering for them as if they were her own.

Did I hear you say, *"Well he could simply ask her!"* Fine, he could probably ask her. But is it everybody that loves involving people at the beginning of his or her relationship? I can emphatically stress, no. That might call for attention of a monitoring agent. The result might be a disappointment. Nobody wants to embrace those things as a negative over his or her relationship.

Remember Genesis 1:28 is still very much offensive to Satan and his agents till tomorrow. Plus I do not dispute the act of rendering such help to one's own siblings, especially to relieve some stresses in the home or matrimonial responsibilities.

Tyranny & Sibling Slavery

Although remember, the fact that you brought him or her to the city (or country) and found them a job, doesn't make you their tyrant. You errand them at the detriment of their souls, as though they were a nothing. This is cruel for anybody to do. Why do we enslave our siblings? We are meant to minister to one another other in love, but many are yet to realise this fact.

That is why some of us do not sponsor one another's ministries. If they are to do anything for you freely, there cones a time when you must know (as a rational fellow) that you should begin paying for their services, in order for the life of your sibling not to waste away. Remembering that age respects nobody, just as sickness does not respect the flesh or hunger anyone's income. Time truly waits for no one.

Let me ask, were you like this ten years ago? One of the major reasons why some individuals in our companies are not growing (thriving or prospering), is because we believe too often that everything should be for free! We can forget that their little salary is their only incentive and helps stop their morale from being busted. Only then can they stay positive and dedicated to the business and it's expansion.

Why Must we make our Siblings Live for Us?

Did you say, *"How?"* How you should do it, or what? Well, it's totally myopic for anybody to be this active. A family where one person is the bread winner is still very much poor, believe you me. Their responsibility is still as heavy as the whole world. But why must we make our siblings live for us? There should be a certain limit. And every landlord should handle their own property as not to cause any disaster if there is no power—money to pay for a service for any encouragement.

Some women, their sisters are everything to their husbands, as if it were their younger ones that were actually married to their husbands. Tell me, why wouldn't any lose man commit a crime in this regard? It takes the grace of God. Please, woman I am talking to you, stay in your ministry to avoid inside judgement. Please, man marry to the one you will always want around you, as though she is chew-gum in your mouth, otherwise be prepared to foster another man's children. May that not be the portion of someone reading these few lines, in Jesus' name.

There are untold Dramas within some Homes

Honestly speaking, there are untold dramas in some matrimonial homes. It speaks that *"what one cannot avoid, one must endure."* Some are forced to take on what they cannot avoid. May the good Lord help us in Jesus' name. Some situations have made some married couples become so puzzled as though they were dumb. Some are even short of words to express their feelings, based on what they encounter or rather even experience in the whole circle.

Hello man, I see you and your trick inside of you. You claimed to love your siblings but I can read dissimulations. Why? Why are you creating a stumbling-block? Why are you creating a barrier and obstacle because of evil jealousness? It should be a pride for one's younger brother or sister to be a great person rather than allow evil to soil your mind for his or her downfall. And you and I know that unnecessary delay is totally dangerous. And that the patience of an individual can easily run down.

An Agent of Delay is the Enemy of Progress

Why? A frustrated element hardly re-gathers the courage to forge ahead in life. If you cannot quickly render any help required by your siblings at the actual point of his or her need, the result is always something else. Why do you promise all sort of heaven and earth by occupying the position of his or her messiah out there after which you disappointed him? This kind of delay is either demonic or witch-craft of you if I may tag. So, abstain before you are punished. An agent of delay is the enemy of progress.

If I say that I love my brother and I am a secrete cunning felony against him, I am a fake, and only God can deliver me. Somebody, beat your mind back to your past felonies. May God help you. If at all, why should competition exist among same blood? You see somebody eyeing his or her brother or sister whereby if he or she is great, are you not a part of the greatness. Those of us who have become sudden messengers for the demon against their siblings for a relegation, repent God is watching.

Repent God is Watching

If you can't help yourself out of the pressures on you or you are under compulsion of something in you, confess if need be for a total liberation or deliverance. So, that is the only way someone can actually step in to help you out; rather than resigning to playing cankerworm, caterpillar and all kinds of locusts against your family's progress.

Stop stripping them of their due blessings. Why do some of us actually make it easier for the oppositions by making ourselves available as tools for a lucrative business for the enemies to succeed us with all eases?

This is to inform someone who can take insight, that spiritual matters are no joke. You actually volunteer to help your family ideally, then you joined member of occult into thinking that with their assistance you can beat the gravity of your family problem but on arrival you became their messengers against your homes. What an irony of situation? Why? I wish someone can understand the spiritual insight over a result of his or her decision, even choice of action before even taking on to doing it at all. Spiritual insight matters a lot. You see, you are now their present reigning agents, wreaking-havoc on your people with any design by their enemies.

My friends, that was a whole complete lot of formula you have chosen to resolve the problem of your family. Ironically, the whole thing has turned completely upside down. Haven't you heard that by strength alone, no man shall prevail? (1 Sam. 2:9) Why then did you not involve Jesus Christ to help assist in the fight for a victory?

Involve the Lord in all your Plans

David did not say he was a fortified soldier, although he killed Goliath and as such moved and started fighting his enemies. Instead, he encouraged himself, even when his men planned to stone him, he carefully asked God, *"Should I pursue and recover?"* And God said, *"Pursue and recover."* Sometimes, we neglect to involve the Lord in our plans (1 Sam. 30:8).

We neglect even to involve God in our battles. We feel we can do it all by ourselves after all this is what we know how to do by ourselves. When a mistake or rash sets in, we will now remember that there is God. Sorry, it is no longer as actually planned by you. You can no longer oppose them because you have involved and committed yourself to their system already. You got it actually wrong. Change from your ways it can't just help you as wrong cannot make or produce any right. Reinforcement with negativity cannot produce any positive result.

This has caged many lives and those it was set up to liberate in the first place. It is an act of taking someone's people back to Satanic hostages. It now looks like you actually become the tool with which your family is now being taken aback so very easily whereas, that was not the supposed case altogether.

Were you under compulsion or even taking on aback? Capitally NO. You were conscious in your undertaking. It was your choice in the first place. Wasn't it? Let's make good choices so that we don't suffer the consequences of unexpected and inexplicable mistakes.

CHAPTER 7

Love of Relatives

Blood Connection

These are collective people brought together from both parental families and by marriage also and tied together as one entity – body even as one family by blood. These are people you can commonly relate with. These are people you can now commonly share your feelings with in a relationship of same blood together without any engagement on the other way round; as they are closely connected to you by blood or by marriage.

Besides the little trust that is now existing among you yet there is still the need to exercise wisdom of God because you just can't trust anybody to the called. They are as brothers and sisters and as such should be treated alike and fairly with the care and love of Christ.

All these are to be done with the fear and trembling of our Lord God with that you cannot go beyond the normal tie of relationship, which exists between you. There are beautiful and handsome ones, I guess you can understand what I mean, such that temptation can emerge and if care is not taken, one will live to regret it. May that not be your portion in Jesus' name.

These sets of people are beautiful. These sets of people are handsome. These sets of people are gorgeous. These sets of people are bulky with six-packs. These sets of people are delighted. These sets of people are influential. These sets of people are of affluence or wealthy. These sets of people could serve as an effizy to you. But you must never be crazing as a human-adorer, because any atmosphere, which can divert the glory of God to elsewhere, God does not joke with because He is a jealous God.

Marrying One's Relatives

These sets of people can serve as pride to you. There are cases whereby one's relatives are so many that one cannot count them nor even recognise them all either. That is why one must ask questions when it comes to approach for relationship unto marriage. Otherwise one might end up marrying to one's own blood, which is abomination before God (Lev. 18:6-18).

So, be close to them and be distance to them as well in this area and that alone the Lord God's name will be glorified. There should be no act of proving any superiority before them if at all. Existence of brotherhood is undisputed and undeniable here. The Lord God that has ordained it, is never stupid. He is not mad. He knew what He did and He is still very much alive till tomorrow. The bible says the deeds of God are perfect (Ps. 18:30).

There should be no sign of any underrating nor even comparison of whatsoever in acquisitions and others; remember your tie of brotherhood. They are your kings people among of whom some will be home base. Some could be educated while some are not. Don't erase their memory even though it is not all about money but in prayers you can also remember them for good. The reason you came through their midst was never a choice by man but God ordained it; take note. You need to respect the purpose and give God a praise. They should be admired and embraced for good to the glory of God.

We can't Exchange Nature

Some of us hardly identify with our relatives, why? Your relatives are your relatives, and mine are mine. We can't exchange nature. Changing it may amount to a redundancy and could attract with some punishment by God. If you renounce home or deny your people of their brotherhood with you, then you have a quarrel to answer and if care is not taken it could attract punishment as well. Such attitude is an abuse to nature. Perversion is an act of disobedience to God.

It is also an act of making God or calling Him a typical liar; of which the Lord God cannot afford to be called none of those names. The fact that you are Tony or Merge and you hailed from your family, a member of that clown, local government, state, country, continental zone, continent and are where you are at present is not all by accident. God is good so give Him a praise who ordained it.

Instead you turned it the other way round. Why do you mate with your uncle's daughter? Some relatives are single ladies whose marriages are being sold in the kingdom of darkness with or by cousins in that they can never marry again in the rest of their lives.

Why? The fact that you are relatives and united families does not mean you should contract. Why are you a boy-friend or a girl-friend to your cousin? You are ashamed with an outsider right, is that not so? And so you want to hide-and-seek the issue. Name of brotherhood is your umbrella to indulge in the act.

Repent

Really, no human suspect is forth coming on your way owing to that you felt you were quite free. You are not exonerated as far as God is concerned and so you must be punished for it. Repent for the Lord God is watching. We cannot all hide it from God (Heb. 4:13).

Why did you steal the emotional heart of love of that your relative you dis-virgin in that if she does not negotiate with you she can no longer settle down? Why did you steal her heart? At least, release her heart so that she can love her future spouse; even though the damage has been done already. For crying out loud, *"A child should be left to cry after a beating, in order to express his or her feelings."*

Except by God's Intervention

Physically and spiritually, I have personally observed it with some elements that there is little or nothing anybody can do about the intercourse actually existing between some relatives except by God's interventions. Some of them are actually spiritual husbands and wives and boy-friends and girl-friends and as if something has tied them together like a knot in that no human solution can stop it any more, somebody needs mercy and the deliverance of God.

Is that the reason why you are relatives? They are supposed to be your gold, to the glory of God. You should feel one another without things falling apart. Change and turn up a new life, so that your dealings can give God a praise.

Why did you organise the children of your late brother to be stealing for you? Why didn't you use your own? If at all, it is even good, *"An eye can actually feel the pain when the thumb is driving it."* If, peradventure anything happens to them, you did not lose, you concluded. Is that not why you don't bother using them in that manner? Of course yes.

Self Interest

Remember God is watching. Outsiders that have no good eyes concluded that you are so very generous on seeing you around your late brother's children; not knowing that you are using them dubiously for your enrichment. I pity your selfish interest. The girls you sent for a prostitution, to be making money for you because you are over fascinated, are not a hidden case before God. Some will fall sick, which you partially show concern relatively with treatment or without.

God will deliver you. But tell me why you should act like the *"fowl that roam with the available chicken, without bothering about the rest"* at the end of the day. And the old man you gave your late brother's daughter, would you have given her to him, if she were your direct daughter?

They have made you a semi-advance agricultural because you succeeded in making them your labourers in your farm business. Sit down and reason very well, do you really have conscience? Let me talk sense into your head. It is not all about being a man with a family.

No Man Escapes His or Her Reward

Do you know what? You need deliverance and God's genuine help, without which you just can't do any good. One can only produce good based on what one has from within. Know fully well, that whatever you do to a child lingers long in him and even grows with him.

Be careful, because you are not going to be strong forever. These are people that will talk about your history. If you threaten them now, they may keep quiet as if they don't have any say. Whatever you do, the public must hear of it in due time; I berth you. And besides, your children you tend to protect and pet with high esteem may suffer part of the consequences. No man escapes his or her reward.

No matter the crave of the affairs of this world, take it easy or else you are just creating a disaster for yourself in the prospect. If you don't mean anything good for the young generation, life will turn against you. In case you don't know, I will tell you, nature does fight when things go wrong with humans as a result of perversion.

CHAPTER 8

Love of Parents

Highly Respected

I thank God that it is lately becoming a reigning thing in the entire globe, that father and mother are very important; celebrations for father's and mother's days are highly respected nowadays. Some are even taking it beyond that level as far as celebrating birthdays. This is good, to make them feel at least human. Life with the blink of an eye! If we do have, we all should endeavour to take good care of our parents. I tell you it gladdens the heart of God.

Some can even celebrate their birthdays now and happily live their lives just to feel like someone. We also thank the Lord God for the religion of Christianity that He has provided for us, as a holy civilisation in which Jesus Christ is the head. In the churches of Christ, believers have been inculcated with a Spirit of true love for their family members, mostly their fathers and mothers. He-God has attached it with blessings, if we should respect our parents (Ex. 20:12).

It shouldn't be idol in our society anyway. Please, don't worship your parents though, or else God may not take it likely with you. Do the normal thing, with the right motive to the glory of God. If by obligation, *"we must unite, we are therefore not asked to contract."*

Some worship their parents and thereby offend God. The fact that it is now a part of our practices, doesn't make it an idol to worship, because His Sovereignty hates idols with a passion, (because He won't share His glory).

Nothing is Taken for Granted

Christian's holy culture does not overlook everything. This is because our Lord has a pattern by which He has said we all should praise Him. In the deliverance department in the churches of Christ, nothing is taken for granted. They hold on to it with all high esteem. If you realise there are abortions and emitters, you must respect your parents who caused you birth. It would have taken just one tablet, and you'd have been gone as a foetus. God is great. Praise be to His holy name, who encouraged them to bring you down safely.

What about other semen in your father's testicles that were wasted as a result of fun by sex? Don't you rather think you could have as well been wasted just like them? Then you should thank the Lord God who specifically preserved yours until it resulted in your foetus, which birthed your person.

Hunger was humanly enough as an excuse to terminate your pregnancy by them but it didn't happen. Instead, God fed them and made sure you were comfortably brought down with success. We must say a big thank you to the most great provider and giver of life, the Sovereign Lord God Almighty.

Honour but don't Worship your Parents

That is why God commanded that we should honour our parents. He—God did not stop there but simply went further as to commanded us with a condition that if we obey them, we will enjoy the benefit of the blessings thereof and that if the reverse is the case, it would incur us with a curse (Ex. 20:12). But they must never be allowed to take the place of God in our lives (Matt. 10:37).

I pray for someone, every personal or generational curses (as a result of disobedience to parents) be nullified in your life, in Jesus' name.

They gave birth to us, and that is what they know about us besides the responsibilities that follow; meanwhile God is the ultimate Landlord. They could be close to accurate knowledge about our destiny but not the whole. Salvation is personal that's why (Phil. 2:12). And so, we all must learn to be distinguished, mostly when it comes to respecting our parents. We must know that parents are actually parents, while God is God. Some of us base our respect for our parents on social status. May the good Lord help us.

Stop Shying way from your Responsibilities

The fact that your parents did not go to school doesn't mean you should begin to disobey them. The fact that they are not very rich doesn't mean that you should begin to disobey them. Why do you prefer only to honour and respect those handsome parents of another person to yours? If they are looking for you they always find you in that beautiful compound or house rather than your own house—mould, tent, hut, ordinary cement-block building yet to be plastered.

The fact that your house is yet to be fenced does not mean you should always run away from the house by shying away from your responsibilities. Whether it's necessary or not, you are not always available. Why do you shy from your originality at the moment? Does that mean you are going to remain like this forever? Due to the present family standard, you are ashamed to identify as a member of that home.

Who knows, you could be the one to change it for the better when God blesses you tomorrow. Renovation or innovation can always take place for a better. You can even begin by having the dream that you are the one that would effect a positive change in your family house, to raise the standard.

Greater than your Parents

Let me ask you a simple question, as your parents caused you birth won't you love to in-turn birth them? That is the golden prayers of every responsible parents to their children. I pray for someone who is reading this book right now, that by the power in the name of Jesus, you shall be greater than your parents. The prayer of parents goes a long way in helping God in the life of a child, the bible says.

Someone should tell me, is it by disobeying them that you would secure a blessing or they themselves would have the heart to pour you with blessings? Absolutely not. Do not colour their graves after death as they are alive, do to them as children would to parents. God is watching. Give them good homes, clothe them, feed them and clean them up. Do what you can, for it is possible that you may not really been able to do it all; God understands you will never be prosecuted in heaven in Jesus name and you will be blessed for it. Give them a call and pet them. Let them feel you for good as children. Pay them a visit occasionally.

Disfigured by Parental Negligence

We know that one individual history is different from another. Some of us have scars due to parental negligence over us when we were just in our teenage years, when they were caring for us. Disfigured faces, hands, eyes, ears, mouths, breasts, legs, and skin (with inability to turn normal) are the order of the days. Finding a life partner becomes so very difficult due to a part of our body, which doesn't look any good, normal and beautiful like others.

Human distinction is another thing entirely. Secondly, it is hard to please humans with choices. May God help us. When one looks at themselves, one almost disowns their parents. The fact that it happened like that doesn't mean you should abuse their parenthood over you.

Honestly, some parents must be questioned to order. Asking, *"Why?"* The reason is that whatever is humanly exhibiting question-ability among the human race today, is generally responsible by parents.

Left to Fend for Themselves

Question marks in our human society is responsible by parents to some extent. Many children have relatively little or no parental care. You can imagine from teenage-hood, a child lacks his or her parents. It's just like a mother hen or a fowl who has lain her eggs without any incubation, (not that the parents are not alive; they are very much alive). Maybe it's due to some other factor instead, like the couples are no more and as a result everything goes haywire. Then some young children are left to fend for themselves.

Many orphans find it so very difficult to live to survive this. It is either they lost their parents to death or have a ghost, mistaken as a mother, who birthed them and then dumped them at the wayside for some other person to take to the orphanage.

There is a difference between being raised by foster parents and real biological parents. Inexperienced children in the world are always tossed to and fro. Because, most of them lack education. In every opinion or forum, the contribution of anybody will determine who has been humanly trained up or been raised. I wholly put it before us all, that parents are to share from the blame of bad government in the whole wide world.

Attention please, the fact that some parents failed does not grant you any right as a child with the certificate of abuse and permission to underrate them. It doesn't grant you with any permission or privilege to mess with them else you incur a curse and you still have quarrel to answer with God. Don't use them for a ritual.

Ritualism & Pretentious Love

The reigning crime people only show their parents pretentious love when they are about to use them for a ritual, why? That so called father of yours, whom you never regarded, was the one you used first for a ritual, but he didn't do it. He simply took good care of you, sponsored you through school, without engaging in any of those form of negative orientations of yours.

Today you say he's a fool, who doesn't know what he's doing. So now, he's just a tool for ritualism, for your enrichment overnight. May the good God deliver you. You felt now that you are wiser; nay not knowing what an elderly man sat seeing, who travelled around the world, a child can't see it. God will judge and help you out of being over-inclined with evil as a ritualist.

God will Judge our Actions

Guy, why did you embrace your mum for an intelligent ritual, which only you know what you did. If spinal drop, you will be the one to first cry out tomorrow, don't pretend to be unaware of what killed her. You sold for money and yet turned around to share tears, why? My friend wipe your tears and recalculate your memory, now you can remember when, where and how, as such don't pretend crying instead go and pray for mercy and forgiveness of God. Inhabitants of the world give them kudos on their doings. But God will judge.

It is actually good to love parents because they brought us to this world, by God. We originated through them. Eventually all of us are each replicas of our parents. They care and provide for us. Whether or not a child is fine, good parents must like him or her. They taught us about life generally, the do's and the don'ts. Even before I started my Christian life, the advice my parents used to give me then, have been a confirmed knowledge extracted from the scriptures, unknowingly to them. But these were parents without even the minimum of an elementary education.

Anointed Advice

Secondly, the majority of parents were not Christians. Surprisingly God used them anyway, with anointed advice and discipline to make impart in us. To this end, I must say, *"Well done parents, without correct education; God blesses you."* Until tomorrow, there are things pertaining to that advice that I can no longer go against, or disobey, since it corresponds with scripture. And with the anointing of God of their advice, it has stuck in my memory, and even formed part of my character.

Teach a child the way he or she should go so that when he grows he will not depart from it (Prov. 22:6). *"In fact, there are things even when pressurised with a gun to my temple,*

I just can't do. God be praised. God is good and may His name be praised," said Helen Jet.

Initially, good quality advice and discipline from genuine parents can be regarded as hard wickedness by the children but in the long run, (as one begins to get insight and becomes inclined with the whole thing), one begins to embrace them by and by. And discovers that without their parent's help, they would've turned out a complete nuisance to society.

Admit there were times your Parents knew Better!

"I would have been something else in character if not for my father's intervention," said Veamon Cattle. *"I can remember how I used to sneak out with a friend just to learn how to smoke cigarettes. Until one day, my intelligent father caught us and that actually marked the end of the whole game,"* related Shaggy Newton. Sometimes, the young would think that they are smart, not knowing that adults got their senses under their fingernails!

At times your parents may not want you to come out, for an inward reason, unknowing to you. All you are expected to do is just simply obey. It is for your own good. It might not be an act of caging you, but may actually be a reason of protecting you indoors for your good. Outside might be dangerous at a particular point in time, you can't tell. You must admit that in certain issues, your parents actually knew better. For example, Noah and his family were shut in by God, until the danger outside was over (Gen. 7:16).

Don't Incur a Curse on your Generation

No matter the situation, except by witchcraft, parents can never pretend for their child to be destroyed, no, never. Considering the process a woman goes through to have her baby, someone cannot think that such can happen except by witchcraft. No one watches his or her property be destroyed, let alone children that money cannot buy. Be wise. Not until your parents can now confide in you that you are now matured with senses and so have minimum or no risk of fear at all about you they may not give you extra freedom with trust.

We know that some parents are arbitrary. They may be smoking and drinking even abusing alcohol defiantly and yet actually asked you not to. But that does not mean you got the impetus to disobey their order, whereby they are actually right beside the pain it cost them to give you birth. So, be-careful on how you treat them as not to incur a curse in your generation.

One can agree with me that parents are heads over their children in any family. And that they are as well vested with certain authority by God from on high to care and preside for the family needs. Good parents are conscious when things are good as well as when things are bad. As children, you are subject to them. As they brought you to this world, then they ensure that you are well protected.

Demonic Acquaintance

Under compulsion, some parents have been lured to embark on diabolical means with charms, as a measure of protecting their children against any attack by a demonic acquaintance. And as such they go extra miles to dedicate you to juju, native doctors and even river spirits, based on their ignorance and wrong advisers. Demonic acquaintance, may the good God that created the heaven and the earth punish you according to (Zech. 3:2).

We all need deliverance today; it was the fault of parental mistake in s attempt to protect us, which was the direct result of wrong advice. It was the orientation they got from acquaintances to protect their children before they got salvation. Do you know a mother hen or fowl? If yes, that is exactly what I am talking about. A mother hen would brood over her chicks, after much roaming, for protection against hulk and predators.

Sometimes your parents will go to bed with an empty stomach while they make sure you are filled. You may not seem to realise this. Yet that would be the most time you fight your siblings over their little offences against you. But I thank God you were fed even though you abused the care, because you did not actually know the value of it nor how far your parents went to provide the food which gave you energy; as such you abused it.

Rebelling Against Parents Never Ends Well

All hail parents. They must effortlessly fix things together for the children, no matter what. Thank God for knowledge, if not this golden opportunity wouldn't come your way. Even though they might be indulging in what they actually advise you against, you must never rebel against them.

Desist exactly as advised by them, for you may hardly know the implication of some irrelevant strong headedness.

Some of us do abuse our parents even, beat them up, why? That was disobedience in the highest order. Please, desist from it, it can't help you, else you incur a curse and accelerate your early grave. Instead, if you can know that there is a bewitchment, then you can as well believe that certain powers could lay hold on them to help ruin their homes by their hands. They may not even know what is wrong with them.

Evil powers may actually be doing something somewhere unknowingly to them. As you can discern, they are going off track and something is wrong with them. I believe you also know what is right to do, as a solution in the right position to help, I must put it on you that you are matured (that are no longer a baby) and must pray to God for their help.

They Need Our Prayers

The leaders need our prayers to do well in their leadership positions over us (1 Tim. 2:2). If you and I must enjoy good governance, we must pray to God that owns it, to release it. Imagine parents being lured into alcoholic beverage and smoking of marijuana, even snuffing cocaine. It was posed in them by evil powers so that they don't know the right thing to do, to actually move their lives and family forward. When anything is projected to actually disrupt your ministry, as a wise person, you must pray to God for a solution.

The devil hates good things and that is one thing you must know. Isn't that crazing? Error should be corrected with right, castigation just can't help nobody. It is a pity. Might be they've actually tasted and discovered the negative impact and harm they do to the body but lack the power to exercise their freewill over it.

Therefore, what they can do is to continue to advise you against it due to the harmful impact. And you know they must advise you against the danger no matter what. Who knows, they must have vowed that none of their children would taste it. Do not sulk when your parents talk to you concerning issues that will help your life.

Some of us claim to obey our parents, whereas we don't. For example, you sell and abuse drugs defiantly and then call that obedience. Whereby your parents once advised you against it. The fact that you needed some urgent money doesn't really mean that you are permitted with any right to violate their parental order over you. To the extent, you would refuse to eat because you are warned against something. Believe you me, if you allow that to be deeply rooted in your character, it might rob you of opportunity in the nearest future.

Harry cut in, *"I was working in one of the best companies. One day I resigned because my MD was always scolding me for a correction on jobs I was assigned to do, which I did not do so very well as a potential employee. Why did I refuse to take correction? It was because, it is becoming a part of me since I was a teenager. I learned it as I was with my parents. I never knew it was going to do me some kind of harm."*

"I Never Knew I Needed Deliverance"

"It became even a syndrome in me from which I needed deliverance and I didn't even know. For example, whenever my parents talked to me, I would sulk and sulk and not eat the whole day. My parents would beg and beg, but no way. At the time, I was thinking that I was doing them, not realising that I was actually doing myself. Until it cost me my first job I never knew I needed deliverance."

Repent, there is no good home without discipline. My parents were typically disciplinarian. If you don't go, you don't know. If you are not in any family, you don't know what is going on in there.

Don't Abandon Them

They need your help by prayer. Do not complicate issues by leaving home. Don't renounce home. Don't disown them. Don't abandon them. I repeat, on no account should you announce them to the world. It might jeopardise their situation. May we not be a spoil or a ruin to our own families in Jesus' name. And so, pray for them. So that, *"strike the shepherd and the sheep may scatter"* will not be their portion (Matt. 26:31).

My father used to smoke and drink alcohol. He never allowed us to taste it. And I thought then that he was doing us, his children. As a complete adult, I now realised the danger he has actually saved us from. I can testify of a lot of personalities whose lives were ruined by alcohol and smoking.

Larry used to be a handsome guy I admired so very much. That if I were a girl, I would force myself on him without him actually asking me for a date! (Permit me to say this, that was then when I was still in the world!) He has incurred asthma and finished himself with nicotine. *"Today I am a happy person on earth, in the sense that as I started going to church, I discovered the harmful impacts and what they actually did to human lives,"* said Frank Kingly.

Gang Life Never Helped Anyone

Gang star life helps no body. The harmful effect is too grievous. Don't copy any bad thing from your parents. Your lifestyle could change them for Christ. They did all they could to see that nothing harm us. Responsible parents must nurture and bring up their children, in order to be proud of them in the prospect. They are the first mentor everyone has before attaining adulthood and then becoming a Christian also.

Parents should love their grandchildren as well as their children. But due to the fact that love amongst the human race is usually not genuine, evil parents can sometimes base their love for their children (as a calculation to juxtapose in order to know which of them is most lucrative!) as it serves for money ritual by intimacy or to sacrifice in the coven.

Parents are Humans Too

As the devil is subtle, he is looking for the one you love most, to demand, in order to have you run at a loss. Who knows, the one they may kill if permitted by God might be a president in the prospect. The question is, how do we practice love? If you love, you are in trouble: if you don't love, you are not free.

Did I hear you asking, *"What of a situation whereby parents egg one of their children into a wrong marriage?"* I have seen many. You are quite correct. And that sounded an intelligent question, I must confess. Do you know what, parents are humans just like you and me, they have imperfections. You as an adult must know what is good for you at any time.

For example, if you notice that they are misguiding or misleading you on something, you must calm down and let them know why their decision is not too good for you. (And I also know that it is a whole lot of war to voice out your feelings in some families!)

No matter your position as a son or daughter, the picture of your babyhood is still in the mind of your parents; for that reason, you are shot down immediately because a baby doesn't have any say.

Misguidance

Even at that. The fact that it is hard on you to express your feelings does not mean you must accept any offer or even allow anybody to dictate to you. If you can't win their heart, look for an uncle or aunty to help you and talk to them for good, so that the issue can be resolved amicably. You must also pray to God for help, without which there's no way. You must remember the devil doesn't want you to win for Christ.

Many single mothers are victims of parental misguidance (into a wrong marriages). You should please, forgive them.

You can still turn up a new life. All hope is never lost. While some of us were equally stubborn to our parents when they were trying to stop us from following those one week ice-cream future partners, we didn't hear also!

Listening to parental advice about possible future partners was perceived as *"caging,"* (not knowing they were actually helping us). And taking parental advice on this issue today, is still considered *"old-school!"*

Yet one thing about parents is that they could see and sense danger ahead of their children and then try to correct the error by advice, parable or even a total restriction if necessary. If you then prove any act of stubbornness they leave you to taste it. At last what you were hiding at the long run they will be the ones to settle it.

Parents Provide Protection

This is to tell you that if you are a thief, your parents once passed that stage. If you are a cheat, your parents once passed that stage. In short, any method you feel like applying in living your life, they knew it even before you were born.

I believe you are touched with some reflections now as you read this book. Why did you actually follow lover-boy upon your parents efforts to dissuade you from falling victim? Yet today, it has turned out a collective responsibility, in the sense your parents now feed both you and your children, why? *"Oh! How I wish I took their advice,"* you say in your mind now.

Your parents must even have told lies to protect you against some dangers and harm. You might not have known it because they wouldn't tell you details. Babies are not trusted with details about truth or in keeping secretes as well. That could probably be the reason why your parents never told you everything. Babies can never be trusted with dangerous truth.

One thing about enemies, whenever they see something in the spirit and then decided to aim at their target, if you don't tell them they must doubt it physically no matter what. Moses' mother did it for God in order to protect little Moses, a saviour of the Israelites from slavery in Egypt to their promised land in Canaan (Ex. 2:2).

Today you can see the result of a wrong decision without parental concept. Attention please, get me right, the purpose of this text is for the one in present pain to roll back their minds, to know where lay the mistakes of their past decisions, which landed them in such an undesirable place.

Using One Against the Other

The fact is this, whenever problems arise in our lives, the very first action we take is often the casting blame and pointing accusing fingers at others. But how can we be certain they're responsible? You see, you don't even know and you can't tell, who is who. So, be careful so that you don't abuse your angel. And I believe you do know what that means? Who will help you again if you offend your angel?

In the past, you have accused people of witchcraft for just no genuine reason. Worst of all, you did it to even your parents and your loved ones. Even when you later realised that they were ignorant to your so called assumption or insinuation, you feel too big to go back to them and apologise.

One more thing, we must know a parent whose advice is genuine and the one who misleads us for his or her advantage, even for a selfish interest. We also know that a parent can form a team with the children against the other. Can't you settle your parents, rather than side with one against the other. Some mothers only listen to their sons or daughters overseas. While some fathers are like birds with extra feathers to be able to fly higher (like birds of roses, you can say that again). Once they collect international currency and exchange it, the next thing is to organise flexing with women and that you know can tear a family apart.

In Order for Peace to Reign

Why do you prefer your mum to your dad? It took two of them to bring you down safely. Why? If one is acting contrarily to their matrimonial obligations, I suggest you go into prayer, to help the situation. You can even fast over it because you want settlement, in order for peace to reign. You can as well engage with them, in a kind of heart to heart talk - with the Holy Spirit helping you. Since you are going for good, the Lord God must guard you up and even protect you.

Some parents accept money from a fake proposal and then pressurise their daughter or use force on her to follow. He or she will undermine the inconveniences it is going to cost the daughter, even if the man is ten times older than her.

Whether or not betrothing is right, it shouldn't be done on impulse. The bible says bribes can blind the eyes (Ex. 23:8).

Avoid Compulsion

Please, parents, avoid putting your children under compulsion when it comes to the issue of marriage. Please, forgive your parents if it has happened to you, or if you have been or currently are being victimised. You are not the first, neither will you be the last. Experiences in life are generally repetitions, confirmed by 1 Corinthians 10:13. Perhaps you were not that strong or mature in your faith in Christ, if so then you would have known the way out. Prayer is the key. Faith guided with wisdom and humility can also beat the gravity.

Academically, the course you red was a choice by your parents. You did not like it but were pressurised to take it up a scope. It was not their fault in that they wanted the best for you. They thought as 'A' made with it, that it could as well be good for 'B'— you. It was you who would have made them understand something; with calm and politeness.

Pressurised into Unwanted Careers

Furthermore, involving their mentor would have still done a kind of help. The reigning thing today is sport. Many parents today have pressurised their children to go into careers, which are none of their choices. Because of Ronaldo and Lionel Messi, some parents have made their children (who were supposed to be future doctors, layers, judges, accountants, engineers, sailors, pilots, even train drivers, highly notable business personalities, presidents, governors, inventors, pop stars, super stars, musical artists, lecturers, educators, etc.), to change paths for a career in football.

Tools in the Hands of God

You and I know that human beings are tools in the hand of God. And as the Lord uses them to fulfil and accomplish missions and miracles, so evil powers also drag them to be used in order to propagate work for Satan. The devil is aware that any leader or important personality is a tool for a propagation. In the business circle, they can serve as nominal partners that lend their names in running a business without taking any part in the day today activities of running the business. And do you know what that means? Satan wants to always reach the antenna of God, at least to gain some glory (since he has no single property that his hand has ever made).

A lucrative business to Satanic kingdom is a little carelessness of the saint. The purpose of mankind was to give God a praise (Ps. 150:1-6). Is Satan giving God some headache today by influencing people and to divert the glory from God, to himself? Of course.

The accuser of the brethren knew that if he succeeds with the parents, the offspring must follow. For example, once he captured Eve and Adam, the entire world followed with immediate effect, (as hostages in the kingdom of darkness, Gen. 3:6). Oh! It is a pity, even the Creator came to die for it (Rev. 2:9). Although God can never die.

The Lamb of God

What actually happened was a total mystery, in that God—formed human flesh and blood upon Himself—through the womb of the chosen woman, Mary. For a remission of sin to be made, it required the shedding of the blood of a ram—Jesus without sin. The blood of animals could not really do the finishing work of redemption.

The bible says: *"Behold the Lamb of God who takes away the sin of mankind"* (John 1:29). And that helps to fulfil the word of God that says: *"A soul that sins shall die"* (Ezek. 18:20). And so, as a Lord with the name Jesus, a spirit cannot bleed neither can He die. Therefore, it is necessary for the Saviour to put on a form (human nature) in order to atone for sin and thereby provide the soul with salvation for eternity.

Imagine, that an inexplicable mistake made by a woman, induced death indirectly upon Almighty God! Jehovah has mercy. We thank God for salvation. Our praying to God, by faith can defeat the devil and his agents with their strategies.

A Defeated Foe

Since our Master Jesus defeated the devil, (the power of grave and death could hold Him in hell) and haven got the key of victory; He handed it over to us. And forever and ever the devil is a completely defeated to foe (including all his associates who stand against the will and purposes of God). Therefore, at the mention of the name of Jesus, every knee shall bow and every tongue shall confess that Jesus Christ is Lord, to the glory of God the Father (Phil. 2:10-11).

CHAPTER 9

Patriotism

Home Sweet Home

Home is home they say. Home sweet home! It is very good to be a lover of your own town, place, country, continental zone and the entire continent as the case may be. It might sound stupid to an incompetent; nay paradoxically instead lays with some element of the senses. Meanwhile, it shouldn't be done with the spirit of selfishness or partiality because everybody has his or her exact place of origin. If you really look at the whole thing, no one actually jumped down from the sky without home.

There is a specific reason or purpose for everyone to originate or hail from his or her place of birth. You should be proud of it. Your Creator has one or two things He wants to use you to accomplish there. That means You must contribute your quota to build the place for the glory of God. So I dare someone reading these few lines or words of mine to start making a pronouncement or a decree of a better posterity over the needs of their place for a breakthrough.

Perhaps, sometimes I am annoyed the way some elements react towards their own places or countries. Majorities rain curses over their land. Is it actually good like that? Can two wrongs make any right?

Bad Government is a Disease

The fact that you have bad government with a sick nation does not mean you should curse your fatherland. Please, don't think we the citizens (the masses) are lawless, rather it's been induced on us by greedy leaders and bad governance. It has happened in the past where scripture says, as the children of Israel disobeyed and sinned against God, He then delivered the captives into Babylon under the leadership of a wicked king—Nebuchadnezzar to help teach them a drastic lesson. After that God restored them back as His people with good governance (Rom. 9:26).

Your curse might even jeopardise her chances of any betterment. Scripture says, there is power in your tongue (Prov. 18:21). Pour prayers to correct the errors. We know that bad government is a ravage disease to the national economy. If care is not taken, it can even strip a complete nation not to actually having anything good to write home about. It can as well deny her of justice and fairness.

Perversion is the order of the day of such a nation with greedy leaders. Resources are devoured by her cankerworm, caterpillar, locusts and so forth; stripping agents that render a nation completely nude and void.

However, there are still a few good men amongst the people. Protocol is what held some of them bound as not to be able to discharge their administrations on what is due during their regimes. There are laws without any positive effect on nations. If the laws are not changed or amended, the leaders are held bound. It is an advice or even a suggestion that if you make law as a legislature, make law with positive effect to impart on the masses.

If there is a Problem there must be Solution

No matter what, captivity is not forever. There must be a time of jubilation because freedom is granted. I want to officially make it clear to us that there are patriotic personalities who will never sit back to have their fatherland totally ruined without doing anything good about it. If there is a problem there must be solution. I assure you the tools the Lord God uses to work miracles and solutions are still amongst the living men. We pray it should please God in time for a resolution in our cases.

I decree that our nations should fulfil their destinies in our time so that we all can be part of the enjoyment and benefits in Jesus' name. I personally prayed to witness my country fulfil her purpose of existing as a nation in the world to the glory of God. She did not incarnate for nothing among other nations in the world. And so, the purpose must be made manifest.

It gets Worse before it gets Better

Once more, don't begin pronouncing curses on the land, because you're bruised. If the situation gets worse, believe you me, it must directly or indirectly affect you too. Notice sometimes, that when a situation is about to end, it often becomes worse first.

Truly, many citizens of the world are fond pronouncing curses on their nation. Please, I implore you desist, for that cannot effect any positive change. The fact that you thought when you finished school you were going to get a very nice job of your choice based on your scope with qualifications and be working in the best of the companies and at the end. Nay, the reverse was the case, yet this doesn't mean that the whole world let loose on your part.

Disappointments

Really there were many reasons why you were sponsored by your parents (or whosoever was responsible) for your academic pursuit, back in the day. Yet you turned out to be a liability to them. *"At the age of my parents they don't expect or deserve that from me...over my dead body will I sit back to let that happen before their naked eyes,"* some of us declare. Actually, it is a big disappointment anyway. As a matter of fact, my brothers and sisters, one could be disappointed in a particular target but not in knowledge.

What you have in your up-stairs can never disappoint you. The *"gift of a man will make away for him or her"* (Prov. 18:16). If one door closes by the enemy, another can always open to you by the Lord because you got the knowledge to handle and manage it. After all, there are courses with diversification of professions. One could be self-employed and yet make it in life.

Running in the Fast Lane

To that end, you strove to travel abroad, there you are starting from square one. If care is not taken, your right is denied of you, due to indigenous laws. Are you a citizen by birth? If not, you have many processes. By what means did you arrive or enter that country? Were you invited or did you came illegally? Look at one thing here, you wanted to run in the fast lane, to shoulder some responsibilities awaiting you, but may you incurred much delay instead. What a life!

The pressure of anxiety had landed some into bad businesses. At the long run, when one is apprehended, you experience so much delay. Out of much frustration and compulsion one is loosed to start abusing one's own country or origin. Why? It is almost deadly to have (compounded within one person) all the experiences of frustration, bitterness, depression, confusion, disarray, and total derailment. However, Jehovah is the answer to your situation and for succeeding victoriously (Jer. 32:27).

Let us, if we really have the spirit of patriotism, find a place in our hearts to forgive our countries and even the government. It was not a crime that you hailed from there. Pray for them. If it is well with them, it will be well with you as well. And if you do have enough, you can even say let me go and sow a seed—making investment there for others to find jobs and be able to feed. I believe this will help many to absorb some of the available labour force (and deal with unemployment) in the federation.

Good Foundations Vital to Progress

Majorities of young school leavers are into crimes because of lack of job opportunity. So, providing with them something doing will relatively help the government to reduce crime in our society. Please, be concerned with and care about it. A house can only stand when the foundation is good or solid. If it is good, it is good for us all. Peradventure, if reverse is the case, we are not left out also. Love your place, as well as the people. Contribute to the progress and development of your origin by voting and vote right.

Vote the right people into positions of leadership, else you regret it and suffer the consequences. God said if you trust yourself to a human being because they're humanly powerful, then He—God will deliberately cause them to disappoint you (Ps. 20:7, Isa. 31:1-2). Delight in praying for their good and it will be well with you. Stay blessed and be proud to be citizens of your country anywhere, anytime, any day. Oh compatriots you are good and unbelievable! It is well with you all.

CHAPTER 10

Love of Unemployment

Unproductiveness

These are the number of people without jobs in any given land, at any particular time. Some economists have said that when less than 95% of the employable population are gainfully employed, it is said to be unemployment. One can therefore agree with me that such is the underutilisation of labour.

Imagine, someone living without being productive, due to a lack of opportunity one may say. But how can you feed? How can you clothe yourself? How can you build a house to lay your head against the sun, moon, rain, dew and insects? You can never have any material kept in anyway secrete.

Here is a summary, of a situation whereby labour is directly or indirectly available but lacks vacancy to feature, in order to exercise its capacity to yield any positive results, which activities of production can affect. It is actually a decaying effect, in that many are the people who wasted away just like that.

A Total Waste

Imagine all the people out there who are intelligent, economically productive, history changers, solution makers, explorers, inventors, business oriented, and so on, if they could not get linked up or have any means to be materialised. It would be a total waste. A conference does not maintain it completeness if the original spokesperson doesn't show up.

What if you're the number one person needed there in that meeting, and you don't even have any clothes! Isn't that painful. It is an error of life in general. What you have in your up-stairs is exactly what is needed in the highly recognised production company, yet behold there's no MC to introduce you and you have no means to reach there. Why? I pray for somebody, not to lack what it takes to be present in their Canaan land, in Jesus' name.

Upon being eager or anxious to get ahead, some elements become completely indifferent. Little wander then why some people prefer remaining jobless and like the situation.

There are many causes of unemployment. We shall get to treat that with time. Employers and employees are really posing problems on governments, in the area of irrelevant folding and dismissing oneself from work. They do this and thereby leave governments with many mouths to feed.

Therefore, if any company folds up, (whose memorandum of association is still valid), the reason presented should be thoroughly inspected and scrutinised before granting.

Battling with Laziness at the Edge of Opportunity

Economic crisis is the major excuse by some of them to conceal their dodging of taxes and thereby use the opportunity to travel to catch fun. A lot of workers who left their jobs did so due to certain benefits they discovered would be rendered to them by the government as a result of being dis-occupied. Besides, he or she will embark on a black job this time around, in order to maintain the story of no job (with certain benefits) for a very long time.

Similarly, so many people just decide to be liabilities, even where there are so many job opportunities. Even if there are means to survive, one will never do but prefer to remain idle. Can you imagine! There are other factors why there's unemployment anyway. For example, you see people battling with laziness at the edge of opportunities. If one is not inclined with the knowledge of some spiritual factors, one can never understand what I am talking about.

Powers could lay hold on one without one being conscious of oneself, one will be watching opportunities without taking any part in the class of the economically productive people of the world. Lack of qualification can make anyone not being able to secure a job for him or herself.

By law, from eighteen, one is entitled to work and earn ends meant by oneself. But a situation whereby you did not go to school, no skill acquired from any job institutes, you cannot get a good paid job due to lack of certificate, which certifies you a professional in the field of your claimed. The only vacancy you might likely gain employment is either of the following: security, a gate-man, cleaner, driver, sometimes assisting the cooks, babysitter, a service to a brick-layer, messenger, etc.

The Many Reasons for Unemployment

We do not mean that there are no jobs, but that they just can't give you any sufficient means to meet up with your required standard. Those with qualifications (without jobs) and who are happy that there is no job, are the ones we actually talking about here. As we proceed, we must try to understand the reasons for unemployment.

Many factors have caused unemployment in the world society. Basically, older generations believe in giving birth to many children. We all know that any healthy woman, free of problems (internally or externally) can birth a village! This popular belief and the executed actions in the past, being carried out by our fore-parents, is the present global trend today as a collective responsibility; believe it or not.

There is no nation today, which can comfortably cater for its citizens completely and conveniently without complaining of one problem or the other. Population is the problem of any family, quarter, community, local government, state, country, continental zone, continent and even the entire globe, on the basis of employment. Somebody answer me, when the supply of labour is more than the demand, unemployment is usually the cause.

Replacing the Human Workforce

Instead of labour intensive some companies adapt to the uses of capital intensive. If where human beings are to work, robots and other machines or machineries are now being used and controlled by computers in the offices, people can be forced to remain unemployed. Tell me how people can actually get jobs when machineries are being used in place of human beings? Lack of information can pose a great problem of unemployment.

No light, no network and transportation problems can make someone painfully unemployed. If an agricultural system is actually taking it full system, as designed ideally, then employment opportunities can even be more than the population density of the supply of labour force.

Pride can cause unemployment to anybody in society. This section of the human phenomenon has different categories. This will prompt analysis by taking us to the types of unemployment.

Various Types of Unemployment

Unemployment could be voluntary or involuntary. This is commonly rampant among junkies. In the western part of the world, a lot of people are drug addicts and it is their job, hence it favours them, they therefore refuse to work to support the pulse of the government by not paying taxes. And no responsible employers will employ them into their companies due to their abnormal behaviours and bad characters. They will hardly befriend someone even within a short time without trouble. Instead they are resigned to living parasitic lives.

They now end up feeding on the resources of others who are law-abiding, who are working and earning by doing the correct thing. Honestly, they are actually benefiting indirectly through government offers of services, without yielding back with any return contribution. They are pests in the society, in the sense that they eat and destroy the rest, the remnants. Since the world is corrupt, they are still the ones people applaud, despite their heinous crimes.

A Demonic World System

What baffles me is that they are the ones dictating to the nations, through their societal acclaim with power from the political Left. Some directors of companies are the foundations behind their powers. They'd rather fuel and oil some of the crimes as instigators. They initiate some strategies for the operators and their co-operations are deeply rooted in the spiritual realms of a demonic world system.

Mafia Law

There is no power except Almighty God; without any back up, back-bone or foundation. If you notice, those deeply rooted in such crimes within our society, got their certificate to operate, under the authority and law of the mafia. All these take place indirectly anyway. And if you are not observant, you can never know.

A notorious criminal can never work; already he or she is being declared wanted. Upon one crime, they indulge in another. If he or she is caught, they organise another. Therefore, simply establishing in a particular place, in order to undertake any good job or business (for a living), is a completely forgotten issue.

It all depends on where and how they're recruited next that determines what they must do. Whether a fellow will quit a particular crime or not, depends on where he or she is being initiated by demonic powers.

Wherever your resources exist, there your mind will be also. Critically taking a view of crimes in the highest order in our society, I find out that the initiation which one receives from foundation up, is actually what determines the act in the manifestation.

Moreover, other spiritual recruitments are also noted to be responsible. What he or she carefully does is to keep on robbing, provided they're able to survive. Wherever he or she is able to reach, the next thing of course is naughty business. He or she just doesn't care what they're able to do legally for a living.

Agents of Crime

In the criminal world, there are physical and spiritual criminals. So, he or she can be either or both. Assassins are in business with the undertakers. The indulgences live on killing and assassinating fellow humans beings. They are usually hired as toughs by the though men in our society to help and carefully eliminate anyone they feel serving as their probes or rivals (in cases of injustice which they practise). No evil man loves to be probed. Actually, truth is a dangerous weapon, which probes to pose a threat on the agents of crime.

No crime person wants a probe. In some nations laws are highly practised to the letter, to some extent, lazy workers use it as an advantage to reluctantly look for work and if they can't find any of their desirable jobs, they run to the office of work to sign up a contract of disoccupation, in order to attract to themselves certain compensations and benefits from the government. Month in and month out, there will be an amount of money, which the government will be paying to anybody in this situation.

Tax Dodging

This has also triggered some directors to flame stories to conceal their wrong motives for suspending their Memorandum of Association with the federal government (still with validity). And once the government grants them the permission for a partial or complete fold up, it means, they have gotten the key to dodge taxes. In that case, much responsibility that's budgeted for is put on the government.

After all said and done, the directors who are the assistance to the government, in every nation, will switch the whole of the responsibilities onto the government alone and dash into thin air!

The Parasitic Life

Naturally, many children of the so called directors do not work. They believe their parents will last forever. *"If dad has done it all, we have little or nothing to do,"* the children say.

If parents neglect to teach their children the issues of life, they will depend on them forever, without doing anything to fend for themselves. They prefer instead to have another person managing the affairs of the firm, for them, once their parents have departed. What a shame, if mismanagement sets in they will all run at a loss and fall back to square one.

Someone asks, *"How can parasitic people benefit from what they did not labour for?"* Well, when they are sick and are treated according to the law of some European countries, they actual benefit. If they sustain an injured or wound one another, they can as well receive free treatment! They enjoy good roads without any contributions. Security is ideally given to them and their property for free and other amenities that are not easily payable by private entities.

Unemployment can also happen where someone started employment at a very early age and can officially retire and remain unemployed. But if there's no benefits or compensation, they're resigned to fate.

Cyclical Unemployment

Cyclical unemployment: occurs when there is a sudden fall in demand. Economic crisis can cause so much of this. Some workers could be asked then to stay at home for a while due to lack of jobs to do in the companies. It might attract (or not) a little compensation. Unemployment can occur whereby one is working with promises of future payment is usually the case at the end of every month.

Workers in these conditions of stress must decide whether to continue working for a company without payment (and only empty promises of future payment). To change for another job or even for a private black business entirely. This type is mostly common in the European business circle. This is why many pretentious workers, when they have stress like this, relent and begin to indulge in crimes.

If care is not taken, when they are caught, one will ask surprised, *"How did it happen and how did they get into this mess?"* All these become the questions everywhere, everyday, in the minds of individuals. It is a decision. Unemployment is one of the highest invisible problems in the global trend. It is a secrete spiritual mechanism that fuel crimes in our global society.

Frictional Unemployment

Frictional unemployment: occurs when a worker makes a change from one job to another. One would begin to ask why the change? Intolerance can make a worker decide to change from one work for another. For example, it is the law that you don't fight in any of your working places. Irrespective of how critical the offence may be, you are expected to take it with calm and report your grievances for a settlement; rather than fighting to defend your rights by yourself.

I repeat, the labour authority says that on no account should any labourer take the law of the work place into their own hands, by fighting a co-worker, no matter what. Issues can always be settled in the office of work. So, you could be fired if you fight in your workplace, especially if you get offended and don't hold your temper.

"One day it happened that I actually got in the nerves by my co-worker. I could not really hold my temper or reaction and so as I fought, I was completely fired by the authority of that workplace. Today I am jobless due to that action," said Jackson.

"I never knew life could be this hard when I was working. If you have never been ejected from your workplace, you can never understand what I am talking about. It is an experience I don't want to repeat for the rest of my life. If I'd have known, I would've controlled my hot temper..." said John Clark.

There were many stories, but time and space fails us to feature them here, to God be the glory.

Rivals who Pretend to be Friends

In companies, if you do not go, you can never know. Histories have been told about involuntary unemployed personalities who were fired from their various workplaces as a result of gossip by co-workers; (some colleagues are really bad to the core).

For example, when one co-worker decides to falsely accuse and report another (to law enforcement), the one being targeted (who lacks the medium to defend himself), may decide to make a sudden change of employment. Simply because it's not worth staying under such circumstances.

Let me advise; some allegations must be evaded before total disaster reigns down on the victim: *"On seeing an arrow, it can never blind the eye."* Many are rivals that pretend to be friends, instead they're your enemies actively seeking your downfall. If you're vigilant, you can easily overcome them.

If you notice a camouflage, that's flamed up of what you aren't, you can decide to make any change of a job in order to avoid future disaster. In some cases, prevention is better than a cure. Fake identity by some other is evadable. For instance, if someone fakes you up and you notice that the company authority is happy over it, then it could land you in even greater trouble. You must avoid that which can land you in jail. I advice you to change for another job.

Nobody wants to Labour for Nothing

"There was a time, I was using my native driving licence, to drive to work. One day I overheard my director say that he would tell the police that I was driving without an authorised licence (of the country my of residence). This was compounded by the fact that he was shouting at me, at the top of his voice! This made me change my job," said Fred. Contrast this with a lack of certain benefits, and this can make a worker change from one job to another.

Nobody wants to labour for nothing. If the contract you signed with the company has no future reserved, as a kind of financial assistance for you, then you can change their job, otherwise you run at a loss.

What if you become old, with what will you take care of yourself? If the contract says one month salary for the company, you can refuse such work. If you got the money in the first place, what was the extent of coming in search for a job? If you are not on a direct contract with the company and you discovered that the agency through which you work is a complete thief, you can resign.

Poor Health Drives Unemployment

Human beings will always have money issues, but who can predict when a thief is going to stop with their over fascination? And labourers can change jobs for so many different reasons. Either for health reasons or the fact that their stipend is such a meagre sum, that they just can't scrimp to cope with it (as a result of too many financial responsibilities far above it). All these issues can birth change.

In addition, some jobs are a genuine health detriment. For example, a worker with partial lung, heart or kidney problems cannot work in gas or chemical companies, no matter the degree of hunger (except he or she is prepared to die). Therefore, it's left to all those workers who're risking their own heads, either to change for other employment or stay without a job.

Apart from that, there are other situations such as random accidents or terrible sickness, that can reduce a fellow below his or her ability to take up any employment opportunity. As such, unemployment then becomes something they'll nurse for the rest of their lives.

Unfair Dismissal Creates Unemployment

A disgustful director would look for a means to fire you from work without any genuine reason. At times, he could pose both necessary and unnecessary work on you as if you are the only worker in the company. He would say all sorts of mannerless words to you, just to provoke you to wrath.

You can be shortened of salaries. You can just be subjected to any form of (direct and indirect) unjust punishment. For example, an agency can stay on top of your salaries (as a middle man), and thereby deprive you from enjoying your full stipend and gratuities (your due benefit), from your company of work. Such practices are part of *dehumanisations* in the workplace. In some companies the directors defy the article of association and become dictators, in order to cheat and relegate their workers. I think the Lord has a word for this situation in (Deut. 24:14-15).

Minimising the Costs

A bad director, who doesn't want to give you a fixed contract (or retain you), must check all means to eject you, in order to doge his responsibility over you. In fact, if he can't (or won't) promote you, he'll want to nail you to the wall, with a nail you just can't unfasten.

Nobody wants to know all the stories of workplace unfairness. The activities always go deeper than revealed and while articles of association cover some, (which stands for the internal affairs of the company), without external scrutiny there's no real solution.

Finally, it is what you are allowed to know that you must know. What of the rest? He and the spiritual associates could come up with a stir of lock-up heads between you and your co-workers; all are just a calculation to putting you in jeopardy. All these are ways to make you offend the authority of the job so that they can fire you. Honestly, nobody wants to maximise the benefits without minimising the cost.

Structural Unemployment

Structural unemployment: occurs as a result of being specialised only on one line of business or job; if the vacancy for that line is not available you remain without a job. Lazy people are happy over this as an excuse for not working or having any job. And so, it is advisable that one must at least have a minimum of two skills, otherwise one will remain unemployed in a case like this.

Unemployment Scatters Many Marriages

Some people do not care; instead are even happy that there is no room for their profession. Due to this, their wives become the breadwinners in the home. Where that is the order of the day, one can imagine the outcome, in a short period of time, if the grace of God does not intervene in that home.

Where a woman that is not God fearing becomes the one paying house rent, (bills, children's school fees, shopping for the house, buying bus and train tickets, school books and clothes for the children etc.,) it will be like a gorilla giving you food; at a time it will slap you that you are demanding too much.

Unemployment has scattered many marriages; most especially the ones with poor money foundations. The moment the man is no longer productive, by providing the families with their needs, he is a complete a nobody, (the present fool); the woman changes immediately against the man. There are some who could not change but because they are under compulsion as a result of responsibilities they put themselves with their siblings and become temperamental due to humanity. If there was no true love before, it is a total disaster. You can say that again. She could even form a team with the children by resigning to fate.

The Powerful Support of a Woman

May God help us in Jesus name. The bible speaks ahead of this to every woman to be wholly submissive to her husband (Col. 3:18) and that includes emotionally, financially and otherwise.

On the contrary, whereby the man is a drunk, nobody advises the woman to start giving money to her husband to go and kill himself. In most cases, when a man lost his job, who was slightly drinking before, will begin drinking more, to be joyous in order to be able to cope with his condition.

Such a man need prayers with love and a good careering. Telling him lovely sweet words can help him to cope. These you do as a good woman in order to help him cope. Otherwise the whole thing is a disaster. Both of you must always discuss the resent level you are in the stress and conclude with prayers and faith in God. One day, the prayer answering God can do something miraculous that you never could imagine.

Regional Unemployment

Regional unemployment: occurs when a worker remains in a place where jobs are down and there's no employment and yet does not want to move to another place in search for a job nor even want to apply on line.

Unlike some people, who behave as kings or mayors in their residence or places; whether or not it is bad with employment, they prefer to remain without making any moves that would effortlessly bring a solution. They remain idle in one place. They are turned author of complaint. It is either they cast blame on the government or one thing or other.

Classical Unemployment

Classical unemployment: occurs when a worker demands for a higher wage. In the real sense, if not for a salary motive, who would work? But the fact that to work is for a salary motive does not mean one must demand exorbitantly beyond the affordable rate of the organisation where he or she is to be employed or already working at a time. And so, if no business organisation or company is ready to employ him or her, he remains unemployed.

The question is how does he or she cope for a time being in a situation like that? Some of the married ones, if their husbands do not work, they may be forced to go into adultery, in order to provide for the family. The married men on their own would be in naughty business nothing more. And when they are arrested, one become so very embarrassed. What is a responsible man doing with a naughty business? How come? How did it happen? What happened that such a personality got himself into this mess?

Hunger can push some people to a wrong direction that do not have a second thought before action. The singles may resign to bad businesses/atrocities and that make them risk arrest, sickness even death. Many men have gone as a result of abomination. May God help us in Jesus name.

If you are too hungry you may hardly bother to inspect the kind of food you are given. Due to being a victim of hunger pangs, Esau lost his birthright (Gen. 25:27-34). A little fake enjoyment can cause even death as a result of the law of abomination. It was a complete absurd to law of nature to sell one's right because of what one will eat and latter pass out as waist. No matter the compulsion, I strongly expect one to maintain one's right. It is an offence before God. Perversion is uncalled for.

Seasonal Unemployment

Seasonal unemployment: occurs also due to certain jobs that usually take place occasionally, year in and year out. In the farming systems, tourisms and others, one can see some of the examples. Employment in the restaurant business is on the high level during dry season, mostly. Ice cream does provide employment opportunities to the concerned personalities during the season, after which the workers turn to unemployment again. Same thing with some agriculture business like the plucking of fruit.

When you lose your first job and you are looking for another, in between the period of searching for another, you could be regarded a frictional unemployment. *"I was once advised by an advanced man,"* said Hilary, *"Why are you hawking and at the same time begging for bread when you are this completed with some qualifications needed for a job by document?"* He asked. *"I told him, I just left my first job and I am searching for another one; that is why."*

Replied the man, *"Son, if you don't like a particular job, take sick-leave for two weeks or there about to try a new job and if you then like the new one, you can then resign from the old one for the new one. By that you cannot actually suffer the stress to have to search for a job too much before taking up employment again okay. Don't just wakeup to resign from your present work and then start afresh in the nude, in search for a new one such decision is boring young man. Am I understood?"*

Residual Unemployment

Residual unemployment: occurs when one is physically, emotionally or mentally unfit to take up any employment. So, any disabled body cannot work in a vacancy which requires standing throughout six to eight hours of work as the case may be; as such he or she must remain unemployed. Some companies do not even have the interest in employing any disable body due to so many prerequisites it takes to employ them, before you can receive services from them. Besides that, not every customer can condone their kind of services.

Of all the efforts above put in place to ensure one connects into something doing. Surprisingly, some elements do not want to work whether or not there is work. *"How?"* The youths of today believe it's a hard life. But they want to enjoy the best! They just want to make it financially fast without minding the cost of supply. Believe you me, it is typically a pest to live like that. That is why fraud is on the high clan as the global trend today.

Tell me what kind of impart they are going to make in the up-coming generations? The answer is absolutely no impart;

for a criminal has no good example to actually make with anybody. He or she can only incur a bad record that's all. But it is a pity that negativity has the largest vote by humans. In human society, everything is a job provided it can put food on your table and put enough cash in your pocket or account, even a roof over your head.

Somebody may say, *"Damn them."* No, you can't judge anybody; leave them with God. If you are allowed to voice your feelings, I do believe you would actually have a lot to say. How can, someone's money be taken from his or her account, without their concept? Imagine a situation whereby someone intelligently removes money from your pocket without your notice and you will be expected to embrace the act.

That is criminal by act. I personally see it as the act of a parasite. Only a parasitic personality can actually tell you how it is with him or her. Some rational humans in our society have tried their possible best to eradicate it. It is to no avail, because populations are on the support to it. What can we really do? Only God can actually and even thoroughly carry out a measure that can eradicate this crime in our society. Evil has a horn that only God can totally crack it completely down.

By the way, who recruited them? Human beings of course; which took place in the spiritual or physical realm. Those that are aware will immediately know that to this end, one is asked to make extra security over one's money, even one's property. The innocents are usually victims of this in any part of the world. I have personally seen and witnessed a situation whereby the indulgences intimidated their equals by age with their acquisitions.

Some are really grieved with these scenarios, even resigned to fate. And that is why you mostly hear the saying: *"Get rich or die trying"*. Please, when you are made, don't poison the mind of the people in our society so that you don't corrupt them, as money doesn't introduce itself from which it comes.

CHAPTER 11

Passion for Money

The Exchange of Goods & Services

The issue about money shouldn't be over emphasised. Nowadays, most people are afraid when you mention the name money: legal tender. The basic foundational reason why federal government made money was to facilitate the exchange of goods and services. It was a substitute of the formal system of goods-swapping: goods exchanged for goods. And that was relatively boring altogether, due to the processes involved in the exchange.

For example, double coincidence was difficult in the whole process of transaction. A situation whereby you have to look for who has what you want and at the same time in need of your own goods; the quantity and the quality are other conditions of their own, which pose problem on the concerned personalities. The type and colour of goods are choices of the buyers as conditions of their own also. For example, a fellow could be looking for white garri (cassava flour), to exchange for his or her yam; while another with yellow garri could be looking forward to exchange his or her for potatoes.

There you find someone who is so discriminative and highly selective as a result the transaction becomes so very difficult. It was not usually a big successful business transaction in those days anyway. A particular product could be too bulky or even voluminous such that portability may be too strenuous and so, transactions with such a product cannot really be that easy.

Money Hawking

People are crazy because of money. They have killed and can still kill because of it. And that must be a complete fascination you know. Ritualism in the global trend is as a result of money hawking. Money hawking is from two consecutive dimensions, which are the physical and spiritual. Whether or not somebody believes it, evil that is practising at the highest order is what I call, *spiritual intelligent ritualism.*

Literarily, whenever sacrifice of blood was to be carried out in those days, they used to kill the animal in question at the process in order to complete the whole performance. But today, they have intelligently featured the act of not killing the animal anymore. Meanwhile, a part of it has been used for sacrifice and yet treated while the animal is still moving with half life unknowingly. Can you imagine! What am I implying with that illustrations? We shall get to a point that I have to explain the idioms. And so, hold your peace and stay tuned. So, permit me somebody to suspend that for now. I shall unveil it as time goes on.

Avoid Money Lust

There is no law against having money or getting any level of riches. Money is good and important. Love money but don't lust for it. The lust for money is the root of all evil (1 Tim. 6:10). God loves money. He—God said bring ye tithe and offering in my house that there may be meat (Mal. 3:10).

When one is over fascinated with money, one can kill or ritualise for it. There are so many scriptural examples that advise man against financial dishonesty, in the act of transactions with one another in all ramifications. It's not as if the silver and gold are not God's.

Since, it is not necessary that God catapults money down all the way from heaven, He has to decide to make do with the ones available in the hands of man. For your information, the reason was because, when they want to buy anything for the church, helping of the needy or some less privilege brethren in the churches, in short anything that has to do with money to run the church in order to move the church of God forward was why God needed tithes and offerings in the churches of Christ.

The Levities also have no portion other than what is got from the churches. And we are to use everything to praise

God (Ps. 150). Offerings in the church belong to the pastor (Deut. 26:12, 1 Cor. 9:13). Remember, the power to make money is God's. Otherwise, the act of raising offerings and tithes are to no purpose.

We already know that money is a means by which the exchange of goods and services conveniently takes place. It is an ordinary legalised paper by the federal government for a convenient exchange of goods and services. By it, the measure of value is fast and possible.

It is a fundamental acquisition even though one must have to work to have it. The statement implies that, when one is coming to the world, one is just a common baby without any clothes on but nakedness. And so, in between baby stage and your last second on earth, is where you need and make everything with which you are sustained by, until you finally bid farewell to the earth. It is a pity that majorities are yet to get this dangerous truth cleared.

There's no Honesty Today because of Money

This is why, whenever some humans are asked to take aliens they take allowance for just no genuine reason. Look! The fact that you should like money does not mean you should begin to lust for it. This alone has posed a great problem in the world. Honesty is lagging today in man with the issue of money. None is honest anymore because of money. Human beings are sold and bought for it. Even wilful slaves openly deliver themselves available as a wilful slave without any sign of shame on their faces in the world today because of money.

If you have eyes, you can see them. Physical and spiritual trading are programmed and equally based on money valued by the traders. I perceive in the second world why human messiahs fail God, on errands to accomplish miracles on their fellows in perversions and in diversions of blessings; no wonder Satan failed God also.

Money & Technology

If a lady or a woman must sell the dignity of her womanhood, it is for money; because she lusts for it. If a man must half his life span due to a cult, it is still money. Money coupled with technology have hatched eggs of commotion in the universe and thereby turned the world upside-down. There is much to give kudos to history and to question this present era. Here comes the question of where is the last bus-stop for money? It does not exist anywhere except by death. It is only when you do no longer breathe that you actually stop to have cut-throat over money on human grounds generally. It takes the Spirit of God to caution self against any lust over money.

If the dead should resurrect, they will still embark on activities, which must give them money. It takes a fully delivered personality to control themselves with the issue of financial needs. Why? Because, the devil has strategies and an evil financial spirit for it. And as a result, if the spirit is allowed to have its way, it intoxicates the targeted in question.

Losing your Head for Money

Many use money to intimidate and terrorise others. You will begin to imagine, *"Is this Frey, my brother, my friend I used to know?"* Yes, that was then. Frey is ready to kill you for money now, if care is not taken. He just doesn't take any chances now, be careful with him, so long as an evil financial spirit is still very much at work in him, with a tendency for shedding blood at any time.

Do you know that inside judgement lies the attitude of mankind in reaction towards money? *"How?"* Fine. I will tell some what they need to know now. I could ask any rhetorical question I am not left out but you need to answer it yourself based on how you are concerned.

Perhaps, if you are counting a huge sum of money within your closet and suddenly there is a knock at your door, in an attempt to checking who is at the door with some notes on your hands; how do you see who is actually at the door? Is it by stretching out your hand or your head?

If it is by stretching out your head. Then your life and money, which is more important by stretching out your head first? Or with what will you see who is at the door by stretching out your hands with some notes of money? (I know there is a hole in some modern doors with which one can easily do that conveniently).

If you open the door, you are seen with some notes at hand. And if you decide to go back, someone has already made him or herself known that he is at home with the sound made to the door point. And so, no excuse. I think the best thing is to drop the money completely and go and find out who is actually at the door. And if peradventure anything happens to your head, don't you rather think it is inside judgement; by valuing money more than your head; or rather you misused your life by allowing it to be sacrificed just for paper currency.

The fact is that, each life has accountability. If your head is gone, the money is also gone, as an advantage for whom was actually hunting for both you and the money. Because you are going to be his or her obstacle to the money and so, he has to get rid of you in order to have it.

Jealous for Money

My brothers, do you know even animals (mostly domestic) indirectly have interest in money? Are you surprised? *"Oh yes, I am telling you the truth about my practical experience with a cat sometime ago,"* said Henry. *"A cat once gave me some finger designs on my hand in an attempt to drag the money the owner threw to me from the upstairs!"*

Take for instance, in Europe, where whites people have pets in their various homes. Whenever a dog or a cat in the house sees its owner giving you something (whether food or money), it's not usually happy about it. The next thing you see mostly is the dog, barking and snarling with tendency to bite you, to express its anger towards you.

If animals could act closely to that extent as demonstrating hatred with the issue of money, as if it were a human being, the jealousness could be so high that he or she could kill you because of that money. May God deliver us.

Money has a spirit which Controls It

Money has a spirit that controls it. This is why, it is possible one gets intoxicated with it. You can see that, there is a need for self-control over money. Some lawless youths have abused and engaged with their elders because of money tussles. Yet at the judgement seat, he or she will still receive vindication despite the crime of humiliations and even embarrassments against elders for just no good reason. They must bend the judgement probably because he or she has watered ground secretly or they have some benefits to gain from him there after.

Injustice & Perversion

Many village elders have gone in rash as a result of this perversion. In police circles, interpretation of law with punishment against the offender is also perverted due to lust for money. Law enforcement agents have sold the authority vested in their uniforms by the federal governments to common lawless civilians in the society because of that legal tender: money.

"Why?" What else if not money issues. Law is defied by unfaithful men when it comes to the issue of money. Some judges have collected bribes overnight and disappointed God. Any nation where injustice and perversions are not seen as crimes, can never move forward.

People have been so carried away that they've regarded money at the expense of their age, dignity and lives. This is the point of perversion where you see an aged person worshipping those who are old enough to be the grandfather or grandmother – because of reigning papers – money.

To this end, it is a complete curse to allow an aged person to greet you like a young person, to you. And you accord to the respect without being conscience stricken. With this notion, appearances and structure have failed here among the popular races. As someone has seen that MDs of companies are highly respected among human circles, he or she has equally striven to own one, in order to earn the same respect. Or even right now, are you just trying to put something together; like a kind of opening venture? You know, that could earn you some credibility. Anything other than this is not counted here.

Can Greed be Cured!

Politically, wealthy personalities are mostly elected as candidates worthy to be registered by Electoral Commissions. Someone may say it is because he or she has money to run the whole system. Not really all that. Primarily, since he has, he will no longer put people in hunger by embezzling the nation's money, (if he or she is able to win). Who told you? It may be so, if you can cure greediness. Forgetting that some kegs can even drip water.

Look at the mentality of some humans here, in that they wholly believe that he or she (because they have the money already) he will have little or nothing to do with the nation's money as a result! Ironically, they assume that the kind of leadership they'll produce must be worthy of emulation; nay instead. Secondly, that there is going to be a leadership of the people with selflessness. Probably, the predecessors might have exhibited self-centredness, (which the nation got fed up with). At the long run, actions usually prove they're concealed with deceit.

Do you know countless ladies that have failed who based their choices of life partners with materialism. The same thing with some men who have equally sold their dignities by becoming men of the kitchens as they dabbled in the matrimonies with the motive of material wealth possessed by their women.

Corrupted Minds

Lustful interest of material wealth has corrupted the minds of the people, even before they are corrupted. To tell you how much this aches in the heart of man, those who would have talked down on mister 'A', (even abuse him to his face). However, if they get to know that 'A' has some assets and money, they will immediately shun it. There is an adage which says: *"money talks"*.

Hence money doesn't talk where it was gotten and so, you can never know how the fellow made his or her money if you are not told. Some elements can go the extra mile in order to make money; more also the respect it earns them among people in our society, bust their morals to make it even out of narrow escape. May God help us.

Preferential Treatment

I also thank God that wealth and material things cannot buy those who know the value of their dignity with God.

Locally and globally, respect to ages has been discarded by the owners, due to love for money. It is a true saying that says: *"If a landlord dis-values or neglects to take good care of his or her property, a tenant can misuse it."* But it is a pity that it is not always like that in the issue of nature. You just can't escape the consequences of disrespecting an elderly person simply because you got the money.

Why are human beings fooling themselves for just objects, which incarnated yesterday? In world history, mankind is older than money. Yet people are no longer themselves when they see money. This is generally taking place everywhere. In families, if the younger ones are making it financially faster or earlier than the elderly ones, you see the responses of the parents emotionally change or switch automatically towards respecting the ones how have things happening for good and flowing very well on their sides. And so, whether or not you like it, there must be preferential treatment among them in the family as far as money is concerned.

Quote me anywhere and anytime, I will tell you substantial reasons to back up my opinion without any shaking. The foundational love existing between some lovers are based on financial motives. Sorry, it is actually a fact that any love based on money is like a house built on sand. It is very much a foolishness on someone to be basing their trust on money or riches. This is because, wealth the bible says could dwindle away as though it had wings (Prov. 13:11; 23:4-5).

When you spend, you do not replace, for example you can't have it back to some extent. *"You can't eat your cake and have it back they say."* But my people, there is one more thing here. No one really knows the prayers of the federal government (of every nation) over her currency each why the manifestations in the heart of mankind.

When God created all things, He prayed over them. I also believe that the governments pray over the currencies they invented but only God can tell the kind of prayers. Please, analyse the whole theories of monetary love in the heart of man. May the truth of the living God help us.

There's More to Wealth than Money

Ignorantly, many people do conclude that if you have money, you are rich and that you no longer have any problem. Nay, it is totally wrong a notion to believe. We all know that money can solve certain problems but not all in the life of mankind. So money is not a complete wealth for anybody. In wealth, we have health, peace of mind, happiness, joy and tranquillity, salvation, money, marriage with children just to mention but a few.

Sorry to say, you can't tell me that a money missed-road personality, with all bitterness is wealthy. You can't tell me, a physically barren person who has little or much money in his or her account is wealthy. You can't tell me that children with inabilities are wealthy. You can't tell me that physically intelligent personalities, without understanding of spiritual things are wealthy.

You can't tell me a man with family that cannot make a decision for himself is wealthy. You can't tell me a handsome or a beautiful person with money who can't maintain him or herself, yet go smelling, is wealthy. You can't tell me that a man with every artificial possession at his disposal, yet is still jealous of others, is wealthy.

You can't tell me a physically completed human being (yet a jealous cripple), is wealthy. You can't tell me that any company owner, who still deals drugs to support their financial standard, is wealthy. You can't tell me who has money in their account, yet borrowing to survive, is wealthy; something must be wrong somewhere.

So, wealth is a state of a man's life, where he or she no longer needs anything, but rather possesses everything completely (at their disposal and within their limit) with absolutely little or completely nothing to worry about.

CHAPTER 12

Love of Prosperity or Riches

No One Chooses Poverty

No one incarnated with a choice to be poor, never. Nor did anyone incarnate with a choice of poverty? Of course not. I simply doubt it. Even though, at that stage, one is without consciousness. We all are yearning for a good standard of living. It is actually good to be rich, with the good type of richness. Some riches can pose problems with no rest of mind, even heart attack. You can even be jailed for trying to become rich; it depends on your cherubim.

So, it will be a very big mistake of any fellow to want to be like his or her fellow human beings based on acquisition; whereby you do not know the sacrifice he or she has paid, what he is going through, and what he is covering up. *"No dancing dove without being drumming for."* My advice is watch everything before even attempt to move in anyway closer to it. Since not all that glitters is gold. It could be packaging, as a sign to luring you into atrocities, by initiating you or to even completely ensnaring your life and so be careful.

Opportunities

Prosperity induces opportunities. And when it comes from a genuine source, your wisdom will not be blindfolded to be able to think of something good to do with it. For example, who has one company will be able to open another branch elsewhere in the federation or across the shore. Who has just a single building will extend to building another or more even an estate.

It brings more enjoyment to the lucky personality. Such a person can celebrate party, birthday regularly and catch fun. With money, you can travel anywhere. Inasmuch as what you want to do requires money, to make it happen at your disposal will no longer have atom of difficulties nor pose you with stress either.

There is no doubt if who is financially buoyant or rich will be able to fend for him or herself on good foods. The body (particularly the skin) as an evidence must speak for the individual personality to the public, that he or she feeds adequately on good food if not with all nutrients. Sometimes the skin of a person can testify for him or her to the public even without oral talk.

Standard of Living

Adequate standard of living must assure you with a healthy life and a level of money you have and more also the care you give to yourself. A well fed personality will always reason good and even utilise his or her time well; and having time for his family also. He or she could even go as far as any length to having a star role of advice for his or her family naturally and artificially without being bored. And always in good manner at all times without being lippy.

It is of a great immense to the children of this family to be very intelligent. Except by some forces of nature would they be made academically dull. Since the opportunity is there. They have nothing else to think about, other than concentrate on their studies; hence, higher percentage of assimilation.

Well Nourished

A well fed personality hardly grows angry. No matter the condition he or she will always take it cool or calm with due respect. Except by witchcraft or demonic power, should any substantial man raise hand or alarm for a retaliation over little offence, which could be settled amicably. At the long run, in exercising such a big gift of heuristic approach could earn one chieftain by any concerned royalty that is if noted with certain commendations. If he or she has MC or monarch they are observant, he could earn himself with such a big leadership position.

This is also the same with a nation that practices ideal agriculture, which bust adequate supply of food productions to the citizens. Such a nation, I tell you is bound to produce intellectuals at a higher level. The rate at which people fall sick is drastically reduced due to nourishment. The unemployment problem is not that much as far as agriculture is a mother of every national economy. Such a standard can even bust the immune system. It can even help to check mortality/maternity rate. It is also very good that someone is able to provide for his own. And has first of all settle some family truce. And that of course you know is the foundation of peace.

A wealthy person has at least financial peace of mind at rest. It could birth investment that might require more hands, to join with him or her in running the business. By then you have succeeded in helping the government to absorb the available unemployment in order to reduce crimes in the concerned nation. One must be aware, no doubt that it will effect reduction of crime rate in our society. Of course, any good hearted police must gratify God in this by beginning to have just a minimum of stress on public agents, posed on them by the recalcitrants.

CHAPTER 13

Love of Materialism

Gaining the Whole World

These are things that mankind needs to sustain themselves throughout their life span. The fact that Adam was given the whole wide world and the contents thereof to physically possess, doesn't mean that one person today must also gain the whole world! Do not forget that we, the offspring of Adam were in him and on our ways to join with him in order to physically possess the world as a collective body. As such, I could emphatically put it on someone, that the fullness of the world: I mean the contents thereof do not wholly belong to one person.

On account of that was why Adam was given everything to possess ahead of us. The little you have today is even benevolently shared with some other persons based on the law of careering for one another. This is actually the area where the greedy personalities have problem with God. This is because, they don't believe in sharing from what they have with the poor or the less privileged in our society.

Another thing we must know here is any wealth got from any dubious means and negative side is conditioned. Probably, he or she might have been warned against the act of helping anybody with or by it. It might have been that evil powers in form of personalities had even put hands in the blessings already in order to give you problems. Any disagreement in any help you get through humans may not allow you to enjoy the full joy of the whole benefits.

There is excellence in the human nature but when witchcraft is allowed to cover it in an individual, one can hardly gain favour by the person in question. That is why Christianity has come to resolving issues. This is why many people are suffering even when their brothers are well to do even okay with every acquisitions.

Each Life Must be Accountable to God

The same human being can still do you at the same time when it comes to doing anything, which can give glory to demons, witches, evil powers and even the devil. The worse of all, the same human being can still represent Satan the devil in some things. Any attempt could mean redundancy or a totally down the drain of all the acquisitions. The really economically productive people do not have too much in their account. They're always busy administering to the need of others.

Attention please, the fact that one should be generous doesn't mean one must give out all that one has to people and turned a beggar. It must disgust God if you are only busy putting upon yourself with too much labour yet you don't even know nor do you care about yourself, if at all you are lagging behind. You could answer quarrel with God. Administering to others at your expense whereby you are the one actually needing to help yourself, offends God. The purpose of each life is to be accountable to God.

One thing is to be blessed and another thing is to make good use of it in a proper order and that pleases God. Do you know by so doing one actually pleases God and even gives Him praise? Yes of course. That is to tell you the degree at which everyone is a party to the ownership of the global contents. But yet, is it not a pity that landlord is craving and crazy even striving to owe his or her already belonging property?

Jesus already possessed the world, yet that devil was asking Him to bow to him that he may give Him the whole wide world. What a funny scenario! In the same vein, if you therefore are God's you must know what actually belongs to you as a person, without allowing anyone to deceive you or trick you.

You can observe that not until you are trying to wake-up, the devil; demons, witches and wizards, occult powers, principalities, forces will not say they want to help you as the system of the world goes under the demonic influence and system. You know why? They have seen now and even evaluate that their supposed offer to you is less in value compared to what they're particular about you.

Land Disputes

In some parts of the world where government doesn't own the complete ownership of land, it is always a tug of war between individuals on land fragmentation, based on inheritance. Many lives have gone as a result of land dispute. My question is why do men drag land up to the detriment of their souls, yet when they died, it is the same land that receives their corpse, why?

I discovered there are motives why some greedy personalities drag land. Primarily, it is to own as much assets which is as a result of the religion and belief of the people. So that, in future, they can start selling it to make a whole lot of money. A piece of land that could be allotted for a gift or even sold for a little sum of money in some years back is now being sold for millions due to development and as well as the systems of land ownership for such a place. Demand and prices on pieces of lands are actually now amazing.

Confiscation & Fake Landlords

May God help us. They can go as far as any height or length to confiscate a piece of land for money, why? Fake elements have succeeded in dragging land, where the original owners yet built houses, schools, estates, companies even, farms without having any form of fear or a guilty conscience.

"I happened to be a living witness on a land dispute that occurred between someone else and my dad," said David. The person in question knew quite well he was a fake landlord, yet he had the audacity to go ahead and build a house on the

same land and even destroyed some of the plants on it owned by my father. There was no challenge from anywhere. The village elders could not preside on the issue, simply because he acquired some wealth. Human phenomenon respects a wealthy person with high esteem. And as the man had a certain quality to be accorded with respect no one probed him.

"Nobody speaks truth, therefore on the part of my father, to prove the man wrong for his deed. Conclusively my father only mentioned his witness to be only the Almighty God; nothing more. The sad of the story is that they are both late and are both buried in the ground," concluded David.

School of Material Interest

In the school of material interest, people are really crazy who are highly inclined by or with the spirit. One would begin to ask on seeing some compound of some fellows filled with different brand of cars as if they are car companies. To the extent, some are even covered with spider webs. The yearn and taste of continuing the building of houses and estates, is completely endless in the heart of man until tomorrow. What of degrees? Some individually educated personalities have piled up degrees in their homes, so many that they cannot even make use of two till they died.

Similarly, many have acquired skills from various institutions of learning and acquiring of skill acquisitions. For example, J. O. Drail's wardrobe is almost a complete boutique of its own. Some elements can never go to church on Sunday when they have no new clothes to wear. Not until they will have bought or sown a new clothes, the thought of attending a service the preceding Sunday will never occur to their mind.

The Law of Diminishing Return

Imagine, a fellow will own companies, supermarkets and workshops, stores he or she cannot even finish traveling around for inspection in a year. Only you own ships and planes and even private jets. Why? I am not against the idea of possessing extravagant property. The question is that, can you maintain it? It is totally bad to own property without taking proper care of it. Having earned the reputation of one possessing extravagant property, one discovered at the long run, the law of diminishing return beginning to set in the interest.

Too Much of Everything is Bad

Too much of everything is bad. If expansion is beyond the norm, there is possibility that lack of maintenance must or can set in the system. Is it not a sin in that case, to own something without maintaining it? It is. And so, if you have children you can't take care of and if you have property you cannot maintain, beginning to see yourself as a sinner before God. Pray for His mercy and love and even forgiveness. As many that would realise their mistakes and cry to God for His mercy and forgiveness, He—God must forgive and reaccept them back to Himself (2 Chron. 7:14).

Apart from that, any wealth gotten from the wrong source, gives heart attack and pieces of the mind. At any time you remember where you got your money and what you may likely expect, it dazzles you with certain feelings unspeakable. And behold, you are let alone to bear all that. This is a total puzzle because there is a condition that you must never share your feelings and experiences over the issue with anybody outside the fraternity; on no account, no matter what.

God Adds no Sorrow

Such warning you know must behind with certain repercussions or consequences if violated. And if care is not taken, it could cost any concerned body with his or her life. Therefore, at this point, there is no doubt, who you obey is your master. This is the reason you see someone's person will be so very rich but the people are suffering without showing any concern about them. You can also see that attitude of indifference has so many reasons unknown to many. That is why good wealth is necessary. The blessings of the Lord, God added no sorrow (Prov. 10:22).

If for example, the devil gives anybody wealth, it is likely that he is still going to collect it back or you allow him govern your life, your home and everything around you. The simple fact is that, the devil himself knows that what he has given you is a stolen property and so he is passionately concern about it. It is only who has that gives and forgets. What shall it profit a man to gain the whole world and lose his soul (Mark 8:36).

Humanly, the words: *"I dignify those that are worth it,"* actually come from this perspective. Someone could pretend to be in love with you, meanwhile, it is an indirect love for your material acquisition or even your star worth: what you are yet to be or what you are already. If peradventure, there is a way you can put those things behind you, immediately you will plainly see him or her slack from being frequent with you.

Powers have influenced almost everybody with the interest on materialism; in the sense age does no longer count. We are in an era that says if you have physical liquid and assets you are most welcome and respected in our human society. In fact, you are the boss. You can even see what is happening already yourself without being told.

Worship of Materialism

You and I know how questionable characters can be; certain individuals pose a great burden on the government in our nations. According to law, individually, somebody is expected to work to earn means of surviving livelihood and thereby support the government by paying taxes. Cooperation in action like this in the activities can also birth increase of the economy of the nation. Individuals and governments build the pulse of a nation whether or not you agree to it.

Rich people are noted in our societies. What earned them with that influence is nothing other than what they have acquired. This is because human beings only know how to worship materialism. Contribute by work /business for good in order for us all to support our concerned; then we all can in-turn enjoy the full benefits of the services birthed for us by the government.

Love of Paying Taxes or Laziness

Taxes are percentages levied on income to pay by the income earners in accordance to law by the government. Tax is money one has to pay to the government so that she can pay for public services. People pay taxes according to their income - PAYE (pay as you earn). While business people pay taxes according to their profit. There are types of taxes. Initially, whether or not you are working which yields you with any income, it is compulsory according to law that per head adults must pay taxes to the government. But then, it was a big problem to society, to the extent men were scared in staying around their families just to see if they could dodge the payment.

This lasted up to the early eighties. So many people were very poor that they could not even afford the payment. Some children whose fathers could not stay away from their homes at the day time in order to escape the tax collectors always falling victims of arrest due to the children's inability to keep secrets. Many children have caught the attention of enemies and thereby made their parents victimised. When a man is hiding behind the door, the legs are almost out; as such, there's a cataclysmic finish.

When a mother is not at home to stay with the children due to their teenage that is usually the case of the man if he just can't leave the children to stay all alone. Then, if you weren't having the money, they used to carry your property as valued for the supposed tax. After sometimes, it was abolished by the government also.

Direct & Indirect Taxes

However the major types of taxes are direct and indirect taxes. Direct tax is the one actually paid by whoever is paying with all awareness. When you drive on the highway, you pay tax at the toll-gate. When you are transferring money, also you pay for the service as commission. All taxes levy on incomes, and profits including special products, like petroleum are all examples of direct taxes because the payers are aware that they are paying taxes.

Civil servants are aware that at the end of every one of their yearly, monthly or weekly income (as the case may be) due to their contract, the government must remove a certain amounts from their stipends, which is tax even though they may see or not the particular amount.

While the indirect tax is the kind of tax someone paying does not even know. Such is called: indirect tax. Sometimes who is paying may not know what he or she is paying and how they are paying for it. This particular one operates on goods and services. We all pay taxes as a result of the consumption of goods or commodities already taxed. If the purpose of business is profit motive, therefore, one cannot expect any commodity to be sold with cost of purchases. And so, if you are buying, you are indirectly sharing the payment of bills, air-condition, and whatever may concern the dealer through profit in the transaction with you.

Types of Taxes

There are types of taxes such as: income tax, sales tax, goods and services tax, road tax, corporation tax, council tax, value added tax, inheritance tax, poll tax, tax on cigarettes/ alcohol, profit before or after tax, withholding tax, tax raise or cut tax, tax on vehicles, tax on trade marks, tax on television, tax on satellites, tax on licences and so on.

Tax on television and satellites till tomorrow are still very much in existence. It is either you pay the one of television along with light or paid separately; which is either with the satellite or not. Yearly, in some nations of the world, you must pay taxes on your vehicles whether writing them off road by demolish or continue using them by law with compulsory stickers. Any trade-mark is taxed.

Whether sign-post or sticker on vehicles must be taxed as well in order to support the government. Every licence must be renewed at the expiration of its duration. Even some individual documents are all entitled to renewal and so, at the process tax is collected.

All goods, most especially alcohol and cigarettes must be taxed heavily before even they are sold to the consumers. Association can be taxed also base on investment which may bring together under cooperative society. If extra value is added to anything under tax, it could as well be re-taxed higher this time around base on the present value as a result of the difference added.

Inheritance

Money (or property) inherited, can as well be taxed based on law operated by the government of the nations of the concerned personalities. The fact is that, since the money/

property is inherited after the death of a loved one, it must be taxed before given to the beneficiary. He or she is receiving it from the estates of the deceased person. And so, the tax is being paid by the individual, not the estate. While an estate tax is laid on the deceased's entire money/property and this is paid out of the descendant's assets before any distribution to beneficiaries is made.

Chapter 14

Love of Car

Status Symbols

Car is a vehicle with minimum of three to four tyres and above and other devices are used which enable it to move from one place to another. It is one of the man-made objects which is capable of conveying people, animals and goods from one place to another. It eases movement. Car is a pleasure and is also for fun. Majorities today view cars as a yardstick to judging any form or level of richness. It can also facilitate good and bad business in the world circle. It yields to the users with many advantages.

Like for instance, if you are driving, you find out that it makes you access many places you could not have accessed if you were just a common pedestrian. With this, many guys have found it of a great advantage to access ladies of their choices. While ladies who would not have gotten the opportunity of riding in such expensive cars if at all now got it with all ease at their disposal without begging for it.

Attraction

Cars can stimulate attraction from ladies on whoever that is driving the car. Mostly when it is seasonal or the latest brand that majorities yearn for it. Love of cars can make a single girl accept a proposal from a single guy or from an already married man (a sugar daddy) instantly without impulse. Even more than one could even flock you at a time since through one you get to know so many of them (as a flirting guy or man). Ladies have association or union naturally like flock. Their lifestyle is more or less sheep like.

Cars can even make some fake parents to accept you as their future son in-law; when asking for their daughter's hand in marriage, without even bothering to know details about your background, family, occupation and all that. I refer someone to a film titled: "One Dollar" just to see how some parents are fascinated.

Actually we have different brands of cars. Such as:. Mercedes Benz, Range rover, Volkswagen, Honda, Lexus, Limousine, BMW, Audi, Rover, Lamborghini, Ferrari, Maserati, Renault, Ford, Opel, Armonk-car, flying car, boat-car, Daff, Mack, etc., just to mention but a few. These are few we can mention with different brand and make even colour respectively. Each company producing them releasing latest of great numbers of each of them year in and year out.

Advantage vs. Disadvantage

Observationally, every man-made object has advantage and disadvantage. In some nations, it is very compulsory by law that you must insure your car. Against accident and other reasons are why you are necessarily needed to do insurance contract to insure your car. So, on this contrast, insurance companies have equally divided the case of car problems on the highways.

There are insurance contracts which cover disasters: earthquake, volcano, tree falling on car, bridge or house collapse on car, car heat at tree or any object by itself, ablaze of car, driver and passenger insurance contract, car theft insurance, life insurance, and many other insurance covers drivers, vehicles and the road users against problems on the highways.

By carefully dividing the line and different kinds of insurance contracts, it makes the car users easily know the category he or she belongs and the benefits that are attached. It usually base on agreement concerning what the concerned fellow is able to afford. How and what to do if peradventure one gets accident; how the car of the third party is to be repaired or replaced. How one's own is to be repaired or replaced as well.

Based on the systems and protocols, if you cannot renew your contract as it expires, you are better advised to park your car or have it confiscated from you by the law enforcement agents. If your vehicle particulars are not correct, you do not park well or you over take at the wrong places on the highway, you beat traffic, you speed above allotted kilometres on the road per hour, you drive one-way exit as entrance you could be fined for it with a minus of points from your driving licence. More also, an important paper of the car can be taken by the police such that you can no longer drive without it until the fine in question is paid. Otherwise no more driving until further notice.

Cameras have revealed many crimes on the roads by the road users with vehicles, which nobody was there but yet punishment was carefully carried out by the law enforcement agents according to law against the law breakers. In some nations were laws are being practised eventually to all letters, no exemptions.

No nation is fully perfect per say. When you are not close, you can't say. And you can never understand. That is to tell you there are secret weak points in every nation believe it or not. Some nations today cannot even take good care of their citizens.

The believers have equally discovered through knowledge of the scriptures that Satan also uses these mediums to collect money from innocent people into his pocket for the kingdom of darkness.

Asking how? Due to your spiritual dullness and ignorance, you might have been revealed to by God overnight in a dream but, nay, you did not understand. You woke up and brushed the dream aside by concluding, *"it's a mere dream therefore it has little or nothing so very important to do with me."* For instance, he can make you come out from your home, only to find yourself engage in a serous phone conversation, which can make you get carried away and before you know it, you've beaten the traffic. That is offence number one, which could attract you with a fine.

Distracted Drivers

Number two, if you are not focused when driving there is possibility that you can run above speed limit on the highways and the end is still fine. The general accuser of brethren has agents all over the world. In companies, in business organisations, in finances, education circles, in securities, on judgement seats, in homes, in churches as synagogue of Satan's according to (Rev. 2:9), in politics, in royalties, and leadership positions and circles.

The devil knows quite well there are laws guiding road traffic. So he must look for a way to network your daily routes with those chains of mistake and violations of rules and regulations of road. He—the devil would need resources by all means even if it takes him to steal; even though, he actually has no single property of his own. He also knows that telephoning while driving is not allowed by law. And when you are caught receiving phone call or making any phone call while driving, the law enforcement agents can fine you for it. For this reason, we all humanly find it difficult with certain issues in life except by God' s grace and intervention.

In short, we have discovered, that life is a whole lot of battle. But with God all things are possible (Matt. 19:23) but the fact that it is like that doesn't mean someone should give up or rather run away. Absolutely not. Hold onto God—the

Anchor of all powers with the faith of Jesus Christ, you will defeat the devil and all his devices. The devil does not want you to make that money. But we thank God for Whom He is; for His anointing breaks the yoke (Isa. 10:27).

The Anointing doesn't Negotiate

Oh! Anointing does not negotiate by asking the questions such as: what happened, could you tell me the story, where do I start? Anointing does not reconcile with evil. It doesn't even make peace with problems or the opposition party. Anointing doesn't eat bribe nor does it corrupt or be corrupted. You have nothing that can entice it to pervert. Anointing does not side part with evil. Instead, it goes straight to the point by braking every yoke, serving as barriers obstacles, hindrances and all kinds of curses in one's life. Provided the victim and captives are released and set free that is its major concern in the ministry.

One thing is to buy a car, another thing is to regularly maintain it. This is another point we must all take into notice and consideration before buying any car. Whatever you have doesn't really that matters but what matters is how you take proper care of it. As income determines the level of demand, so it is with the buying of the type of brand of car.

It is a meagre salary whatever earner cannot go as far as buying a car worth of 2.5m of any national currency because there is not going to be any future maintenance by the person in question even if the person in question has the means of buying it on higher purchase. In that he or she has to make a bargain of future payment on instalment.

It is a total craziness to go beyond the level of one's income of whatsoever you may tend to do. Therefore, the person must sit down to reason if I should buy this car, how do I feed? What about my rent and bills? If not residing in personal home, how about the domestic needs? How about clothing, school fees of the children? Drugs, when they are sick, feeding and clothing, travelling and holiday expenses and others? What of mechanical problems, how do I cope when the need arises? All these compounded with related problems and many more make people to go for cars they can afford and easily maintain without any much stress.

Like we rightly said before, this man-made object—car, can do disaster such that will even make the owner hates ever using any car all the rest of his or her life. You can hate cars if care is not taken. Whenever accident occurs and there are injuries whereby some people even died and the car destroyed beyond repair, is a big loss to the owner.

In the past histories with all stigmas, many today are going without car as a result of that. Accidents can happen by car in different ways. It could be that the driver recklessly drives and spies at the buttocks of pedestrian ladies or even drinking while driving. Over speeding and neglecting the respect to road traffics including speed limit is a total disaster. A driver oughtn't to engage in a conversation which impairs their focus. You must remember you are not alone in the vehicle and if you are alone, a lost life cannot be regained. Each life is important. Drive carefully so that you can preserve lives.

Take for instance, as a driver of the president of any nation, if you are not careful, you will put that nation in a total disarray. No single life is useless every life is useful and important.

CHAPTER 15

Love of Long Life

Aging Naturally

This is the ability to live a long lasting life. It is a natural gift of life by God with the ability to last long. Before Eve the bible says, Adam has stayed number of years in the garden of Eden even before he had his wife. This is the stage one becomes ageing with many symbols of recognition like: grey-hair, a kind of squeezing drying muscle, dimmed eyes, dull nose, entire face becoming wrinkle.

Apart from the symbols of facial recognition of old-age, other very important ones to take notice of are the characteristics; such as: weak, sluggishness sometimes with walking stick or without, very slow in conversation, eating very slowly, behaving childish, minimise or stop in the discipline level, staying almost in one place all days even pass out urine and waste product right where he or she is.

Now, it is the duty of the children of this personality to take the due necessary care of him or her. This is the most important aspect the children of the aged should please take into consideration as though they were the ones directly in the situation or shoes of their parents. Besides the aspects of mummy and daddy, take these clothes, shoes, bag; I do mean the financial and material care but the last stage also matters most.

Be Careful how you Treat the Elderly

This is the point one has to really show them love with care and feelings. Some of us will see our parents in this condition and begin to say phew. Why? Remember how you used to urinate in your parents plate of soup, whenever they were eating, you would be passing your waste product and they'd be inhaling the odour throughout without complaining; until you finished whatever you wanted to do.

They held you at the end of the day with optimum care, bath and clean you up. Whereas you now grow up and begin to find it so very difficult to identify with your parents. Isn't that shameful? Attention please, the fact that you are strong today does not mean that you will never grow old and weak.

Be-careful how you treat the aged most especially your parents. It will be a pity if the elders are giving their blessings at the end of everything saying: may your children do to you just as you did to your parents. How would you feel if reverse were the case of your handiwork over them? May God deliver somebody in Jesus' name.

The Inconvenience of Caring

Many rival with the Sovereignty on this regard being that they don't want to experience old-age. They feel it is everybody that must experience a situation whereby he or she will be passing out waste at the point of his position or being at every moment nature calls. The fear of not want to be mocked by fellow human beings has made some to engage in it. They want to prove that they are so very neat. Who told you there is neatness up to that extent?

The day a man dies he doesn't even know whether a pile of excrement is hanging at his or her anus. It's just as if he or she was coming to life (someone was responsible for their bathing etc.), it's the same when one is departing from the world. To God be the glory. It is only those that will bathe and bury them that can tell. The chapter is already closed and that is the end.

If a fellow then goes about narrating to mock you over a thing which is a must to everybody, whether you like it or not, that is their cup of tea. The day he or she dies, same thing will be done to him just as he or she did to people by somewhat fellows; already projected elements for a retaliation by the Lord God Himself.

The bible says, *"Babylonian, what you used to do to others will now be done to you"* (Jer. 50-51 and Ps. 137). They engage in fraternity to help them out. Not all premature deaths are as a result of power attacks, please take note. Before you mourn anybody if you have spiritual insight, you must know. I do not stroke anybody for life is individual. Neither am I made a judge over anybody. Nevertheless, truth must be said by those that know the value and who fear the Lord. But it is a fact.

Never Joke with Your Life

Do you know how important you are? Did I hear you say how can I cope with pressure and intimidations by fellow humans? Primarily, individual differs by destiny. That is number one. Number two, ask your Creator: Please, who are mine? If you know and you know yourself so really well, you will never joke with your life. And besides, your life is a complete borrowed property from God which you may likely account for some days on how you spend it.

Nobody got the right to offer a ladle to anyone he or she has no right to ownership. Take for instance, if clothes are given to you by someone and then are offered out by you, without his or her concept, I guest you must be questioned to order.

Then, what makes you think that the Lord God will not do same to you when you play with your life simply because it was not bought? What did your dad do to you sometime ago when you lent his only bicycle to someone to go on a journey? Even though he returned with the bicycle without any fault, I believe you incurred some punishment or quarrel along the line.

Or when a lady fell from a motorcycle at the front of your family house, behold even though she did not sustain any injury, but is half naked and to just continue her journey down home was a problem, so you gave her one of your mother's clothes. Were you not quarrelled for it? There was an emergency that you could not look so very careful to actually know whose shirt you wore, (which happened to be your brother's), before exiting from your residence. Were you not also quarrelled to order by your brother, even your parents on return?

On returned from your errand or school, which you hadn't any means of reaching, your mum as to know whose food is actually in the red plate while you severely battle with the pangs of hunger. As you ate your choice, were you not quarrelled for it? Or probably accused of taking the lion's share thereof. Then, what are we talking about?

Siblings have had battled with un-forgiveness for a long period of time before a bone of contention subsided. If you are really conscious and always with your families, dwelling together everyday, there is bound to be a family truce. There is one natural syndrome worrying eventually everybody in the sense, an adage says: *"Seldom sees attracts dignity."*

Let them part for sometimes and see how one will missed the other. It is natural with some humans that too much of everything is bad. A true love is not in man as a result of imperfection. Otherwise, what is bad about someone seeing his or her family members every now and then? What makes you look like just a nobody before the other in the family is from this perspective. Who has no constant love to offer just can't help it; no matter what.

Note there is a certain stage a person will attain in the family house, only to always receive a shout at the top of voices by his or her parents whenever your assistance is needed in the kitchen and others. Indirectly, that is telling you, *"Look! You're too old to continue to reside with your parents."* This is a tug of war actually encountered by many who went out of their houses just to impress those concerned, nay, only to end up in disaster.

If you are not a matured rabbit, don't attempt to go solo for a separate hole. Know that there are predators. A matter of life does not only entails impression rather there is a need to sit down for a thorough plan before embarking on what costs you: life, money, material and other. If you then calculate wrong hence a wrong result.

CHAPTER 16

Love of Sickness

A State of Abnormality

Sickness is a state of abnormality in an animal. Animals get sick and human too. It is said to be sickness of any animal or human whose behaviour/characteristic or condition changes from normal to abnormal.

Anybody who cannot speak up his or her feelings is not humanly worthy to possess his or her human right. It is a total sickness to be humanly expected to strive to defend property already belongs to you. As sickness is defined an abnormal behaviour of an animal or man, some people love it even though it is not something to joke with because it does not play with the muscular flesh of the living creatures (man and animals, even plants).

A Pretence of Sickness

When the undertaking of man poses him with some stress, they declare and take sick leave at work in order to take some rest as the case may be. In most cases, it is not always true. At times, it could be a pretension for a relax. May be the company in which they work does not have much laws guiding her as privilege to take holiday for that period. Similarly, it could be that the company just awarded with a contract. And that could mean so much work to be done. If it scares them, they can pretend to be sick in order to cover the period with the session of work they feel it is too hard for them.

Lazy people hardly face their challenges and deal with the situations squarely. Because their hands cannot perform the enterprise. Some workers or employees are very trickish in the sense, when they discovered that their newly employed companies do not pay up to the level of the formal or there is cheating somewhere along the line as detected on the pay-list and they just can't speak it up due to prejudice, they take sick-leave immediately to satisfy their conscience. But the bible says: do not use evil to pay for evil (Rom. 12:17-21).

This false sick-leave is also a calculation to indulge in else business mostly when the cash involved is very high including the impression and there is no way he or she could forfeit it. Too much opportunity can birth evil or crime. Since opportunity has come up in his or her mind as a notion to fill in the gap, hence a balanced equation.

The reason or motive for every undertaking is money. And so, as he or she could not just let go alternatively, sick-leave is the answer to bridging the gap. It is only on advantage to the doer when doctor does not check but if reverse is the case, he or she has himself to blame. Government will not pay you and you must answer quarrel why you were not at home when the doctor came to check on you. Secondly, the company where in you work will no longer trust you. Satan can be addressed an angel if he maintains a similar case!

Locally, some persons pretend to be sick in order not to follow their parents to the farm. Some parents also pretend to be very sick just to obtain a sum of money from their good Samaritan: the children for a flexing. Even in regards to a sole business in some nations where law is being practised to nearly full letters; the proprietors are mandatory by law to all placed sick notices on their notice board on each of their entrances to their shops/offices in case of customers coming to buy from them and as well as to avoid being fined by local council authority.

Laziness & Lies

All are liars. Some popular sets of people claim that if you lie about being sick you must actually be sick in order to fulfil the lie being told by you; superstitiously, this is based on their religion. Therefore, it goes that *"if you lied that you are sick, it is possible some days that you must fall sick in order to really fulfil it."* Laziness can easily make some people to pretend to be sick in order to dodge one or two tasks.

The workers that are mostly fond of doing this are the unskilled labourers and as well as the lazy type. Basically, if you are shying away from your responsibility, number one examination they must carry out on you is assumption or insinuation whether you are the lazy type or not. If you are the type opportunity delivers a greener pasture to his or her disposal and you are still looking for manner to fall from heaven, whereby you already have one you are very lazy and only God can deliver you.

The Spousal Relationship

In relationships, many spouses have also used this medium to excuse their partners by denying them in bed. May be this period they are actually grooming themselves up for their extra marital date with whom they have an affair. But when it comes to money issue, they don't say let me hold on until I resume my normal relationship, why we are one in the first place!

Many men have been starved over their due food and property because powers told their spouses to do so. Some men can't just talk their stories. Already they are just like the living dead, over cakes without sugar. It is very very hard to voice out a situation like that. And it is like a culture with secrecy a third party doesn't suppose to know. Otherwise, God may hold you in derision. May God encourage them anyway; the dye is been cast.

Sex before Marriage

Another mistake before marriage is the relationship with sex before marriage. Poverty makes a supposed decent man to engage, since age is not a respecter of any man. May God deliver us. It is also noted even when you proposed to a single lady without involving a bed action yet, if she knows better than you, in second life of human nature, you are also finished.

True, the second life of human beings is a complete mistake believe it or not. During this process, the girl is downloading every spiritual resources, which has to do with the money of the guy in question after which dashes into thin air with the claim that the relationship can no longer work or could not work out even when she tried.

Actions Speak Louder than Words

Or better still without oral, she may even use another guy to push you out without impulse. Action speaks louder than words. As you can't strive in relationship, you will immediately let go after all. Original does not strive; meanwhile things are falling apart. But why? From the very beginning, she new quite well that the relationship would never work out but with pretension she actually went into it because she knew her target of advantage.

Why do human beings deceive one another? A tree does not deny the particular soil where it is rooted; but in the case of human, it is not like that; rather the reverse is the case altogether. Mostly when she discovers that her date is a typical ignorant who is just living on his own without being informed. She would want to deform him and then snick out. Why? When he proposed to her at the beginning was when she would have told him that it won't be possible to attain the level of tying the knot of matrimony. Nay, she instead pretends to enter the road as though she is sure.

Human beings, when shall we stop deceiving one another? The benefits of your cheating, where on earth are you taking it to? Is it not this entire globe whereby the highest you can enjoy is to eat, build a home and to clothe yourself up.

Tell me other things you will want to benefit. I will tell you, they all lie in these three phases of human basic necessities. Nothing more my friend. Let's fold our feathers that make us take or even attempt to take what does not belong to us. Something must be responsible why someone would want to relegate his or her neighbour. You have no cogent reason why you must wreck that man or that woman for goodness sake.

Nothing Happens without Reward

Why is your human faculty on the basis of evil telling you to introduce failure in the business of your fellow human beings? Why do we entertain the evil spirit of Satanic errand of the devil against our neighbour? Why did you allow him to soil your heart for a destruction. Why are you so jealous with evil jealousness that your mind towards your neighbour is so full of negativity?

The bible that says be your brothers helper is not a fiction, in that it is indirectly telling you that you got a role to play for the welfare of your fellow human beings (Gal. 6:2). Not after all said and done have you began to say what you can't do. May God deliver some of us from exaggeration.

Many ladies doing this trick have equally ended up becoming customers to uncountable bad men who later become a problem to their marriages. Nothing happenings under the sun without a reward. Where are we going? Isn't this life with a blink of the eyes. To every element, death is certain; no matter what, let Jesus appear right now, somebody must die before seeing Him. A second is too big for that to happen or rather takes place.

CHAPTER 17

Love of Death

The Forces Behind Suicide

Death, they said, *"is a bad reaper and that it is not always after the ripe fruits."* But surprisingly, a set of people exists who just love death and want to get off this planet!

Deliberately or not, one could engage with the intention of committing suicide. A little wonder, why would a fellow with complete physical life, sound and healthy, attempt to carry out such an act with a total loss.

There are forces behind it. A situation whereby somebody will just wakeup, only to start developing the interest of how to just die. Frustration is number one. Life without joy is no longer a life. What you're living for is what the mind is telling you. Look at your mate or rather your equals. Can you see how far they've gone ahead of you? Can you see their achievement? You were mates as told by birth, how come this is what's happening to you? My friend wake up from slumber. Do you still need a prophet to tell you all these when the whole nakedness of a fowl is being displayed to you?

Please, spare me of your pretence. Jesus is Lord. If you don't do something, the young generation will help you out with their scorn. You are already an outdated element, you just can't meet up any more no matter how far you may try, in order to really strive. No way for you. You just better die and that I believe settles the whole thing. At least to feel something precious had left them when they will have mourned you.

Looking for a Way Out

It doesn't really matter how all you need to do is to eulogise the question, by asking people a bit far from those around you, the particular drug that is suitable for a thing like this. But note, you must hide the reason from them until the deal is done. At least you should go and rest now this is no longer life for goodness sake. Have I made myself clear? I just came to help you. It will begin to rigmarole until it births someday. May God deliver somebody in Jesus' name.

Some people are frustrated in different ways. I knew of a fellow called Zilo; when he got to know as an adult he was no longer functioning as a complete man as before, he went and drank acid. We all know that acid does no single joke with the flesh let alone intestine. All his systems were affected and got damage beyond medical solution. Even when he was rushed to the hospital where a lot of tests and treatments were carried out on him, all were to no avail; still at the end, he died.

Control your Depression

When an expectation is not met at the right time and the expectant lacks the faith to cope in enduring for a very long time, frustration is bound to take place. Awkward thickness becomes automatically the order of the day . Self underrating, negative appearance and doings by judging to look at others to be more desirable and better than oneself can birth frustration and if not checked immediately can result in disaster. If you don't control your so called depression you are risking suicide. Such as: is it this same world we re all incarnated? Look at this and that, they have far gone ahead of me.

This can easily develop hypertension and if care is not taken, it could accelerate an early grave. It is also a situation where you give credit to others and discredit yourself that such can result. And that is cut-throat.

All that Glitters is not Gold

By the way, whoever told you, *"All that glitters is gold"*? And who told you that they are better than you in all ways? Let me tell you, such intention is not the yardstick measure for judging every standard of living.

Now, let me ask you a simple question. Do you know what your so called admirable people are covering up as problem in their lives? Of course not. A pauper could sometimes appear so very good and more decent than even a rich person in the outfit, even in the looking. A little girl of no class can even make up far better to look neat and very good than even a wealthy lady of class.

My friend, you just can't define what clothes cover on daily basis. It is not every time you should expect clothe to cover gold. Number one, that tells you not all that have wealth even know how to use it. A man is whatever he or she thinks he is (Prov. 23:7). So, stop dejecting and ejecting yourselves. The world is an enclosure: a place ordained by God to inhabit by man; and so live on and live your lives to the fullest. The world belongs to nobody—one person. Please, stop self depression it can harm you. A moment of trauma is loaded with an overdose of negativity.

God Never Mandates Suicide

No matter what the situation of a fellow maybe, he's still very much useful to others who are concerned. And his or her welfare is in the heart of someone. If you are in any situation, don't let people loose you to death. Death is a final rest which we all agreed to already, as a result of sin in the garden of Eden. But not for you to start developing an interest overnight as though you were just sent by God your Creator to spy at the world and still return to the world of the dead.

Don't allow enemies to blindfold you into thinking that the Lord God is having a hand in your sudden interested in leaving this earth so very soon. The fact that things are hard on you does not warrant that. And it doesn't mean that tomorrow they are not also going to change for a better. Also avoid basing your wants or needs at all costs, else, it hurts badly mostly if they are not forth coming when needed or due by you. It is not fair.

Trying to Escape Life's Challenges

In death, you are no longer faced with competitions nor with challenges either, which we all know. Everyone has his or her own set of human beings in the world, regards to his or her daily activities. But when you just can't meet up with your equals, you feel heaven has let loose or life has totally eluded you. It is not so. Please, I implore you to take it easy with yourself. And however your condition may be, I advise you don't eat or drink any poison to accelerate your early grave.

Somebody, somewhere out there, needs your kind of person by his or her side, just to seeing you (and that alone) puts a smile on their face. It is just okay by them. Naturally, we all have contracts with God; in which we all signed death with Him. The expiry date and contents of each fellow determines simply the kind of death, which must befall individual personalities. The kind of death that must kill A is going to be different from B's, as the case may be.

Finally, some elements would know that a particular sin can result in death when it is committed, yet they will deliberately engage and do it anyway. Just because they want to satisfy their fleshly desires or needs, at a particular point in time, they no longer mind embarking on ritualism and fraternity.

A Loose Tongue Accelerates an Early Grave!

So, whoever is loosed in tongue, loves an early grave. Tame yours and live long, the bible says (1 Pet. 3:10). I am not saying you should keep quiet when you are to speak the truth. It is the smallest part of the body, yet it is the most dangerous.

However, if you refuse to speak the truth when it is necessary, God may hold you responsible, over the concerned issues. *"The wise sayings of an elder saves, but the stupid disobedience of a child puts his head in danger"*. What usually makes people deny speaking the dangerous truth with unquenchable light?

One, fear of reaction from the opposition. Scripture only recognises the holy fear of God, which the believers are to entertain and that shows that they have started to grow wise. The fear of the Lord is the beginning of wisdom (Prov. 9:10).

The Anointing Carries the Power to Speak Truth

For example, if you have truth but haven't yet received the anointing, you just may be dreadful to speak it! That is, you can't be so very sure and bold to stand what you actually speak, because the power to confirm it is not available yet.

In the upper room, Jesus said to the disciples wait, you shall receive power after that you can go about preaching the gospel in (Acts 1:8). The mystery behind it is that the anointing carries power. This is the internal propelling force the preachers of the gospel carry, which sustains them from within, while doing exploits for Christ, in the ministry of truthfulness.

Sin can also restrict one from speaking the truth. To preach against a crime you are indulging in, is like boldly reigning curses on yourself! When you belong to a group that check-balance everything you do, you can never speak to probe them of their crimes. And mostly when you are conditioned, fear grips your mind so very tight.

If your befit is contrary to the complete truth of God, yet you still insist on speaking it, this could amount to a redundancy. If you are still enjoying the benefits and company that sin yields; you may feel so very comfortable. Little did a worker of iniquity know that jubilation over after afternoon's enjoyment, can cause even years of crying, at the end of the day.

CHAPTER 18

Love of Enmity

Malice

Malice is just to some people as a particular kind of food. It is a favourite to the concerned elements. Every little thing or offence they must keep it to heart and then begin to keep malice with the offender. Even if it is a minor issue which can be resolved amicably, they are so heart hardened that they will never let go nor forgive and forget either. It is total wickedness to act like this. And this must never be far from witchcraft. It is only evil power that can make someone to act like that.

There are still other sets of people who are fault finders. They don't mind collecting bribes in order to be able to help couples quarrel or fight. They deliberately act negatively on their targeted victims on whom they found no guile, in order to destroy them. Asking what the offence is? He or she will either declare: *"He is ugly,"* or *"She is too proud and as such I just don't like her and I will never have anything to do with her for the rest of my life."* In short, *"I just don't like the kind of person he/she is." "But have you really taken time to find out the cause?"*

Hatred without a cause always Ends Badly

That is the question, and I do believe the correct answer would be, "No!" Carrying wrong impressions about any fellow, without a genuine reason, could lead to wrong decisions, even wrong action. Remember, he or she did not incarnate with your certificate as to say he owes you a lot. And whom you hate without a cause can never yield with you any positive result or a good advantage.

Discrimination comes because of race, background, family, social class, education, beauty, history, reputation, connection, influence, position, leadership, etc., as a measure of racism. Ask me who gave anybody the certificate to make such distinctions among human beings? Somebody only looks at your standard of living and immediately get aroused with hostility towards you, for no genuine reason.

If it bothers you brother or sister, do something to normalise the situation. And so, you will not have to bother being stained by it any longer. If your level is too low or too high, somebody must carry grudges. Why? What is your business about the fellow? Is he or she living with your certificate? I believe the answer is absolutely no. Poverty is enough for people to hate someone. If you continue with the way you are going, God might hold you in derision. You may just be held responsible with some issues by the incorruptible Judge Himself.

Malice Solves nothing & Hurts even the Operators

God expects everyone of us to respect those in authority. Don't hate or keep malice with them simply because they refuse to discharge their responsibilities as due on their subjects accordingly. Malice does not correct any error instead it hurts even the operator. If government failed her duty, it is left between her and God Who anointed and ordained her to be in that leadership position for the welfare of the masses.

The bible says that no authority can exist apart from the one ordained by God (Rom. 13:1). They are anointed and if they chose to misuse it, it is simply none of your business. You are not in any position to judge them. Every individual has accountability to God, as well as government. And so, taking the cases as your personal tale of analysis on daily basis is an embarrassment to God.

It is not your burden. You are over busying with another man's case but what about your own? Doesn't it really bother you that you are not personally okay as desired by even you? So, adding another man's will make you fall sick even onto death. So, please, stop it for we all can humanly feel you. And as such you are useful to us somebody. Government is government and you are you.

Sometimes, keeping malice could be good. *"How?"* Take for instance, you have your property, which you normally let out on regular basis like any of your so called familiar things, such as: canopy, chairs, houses, horses, vehicles, property and all that. Instead, they want to always misuse it in order for you to run at a loss in the business.

Avoid Repeating the same Mistakes

Similarly, you will let out something and in turn now be the one asking the borrower to please, return your property. And sometimes, asking may birth a quarrel if care is not taken. And so, the advice is, instead of continuing to let your property out, every time at the risk of losses or incurring a misunderstanding with the concerned person in the transaction, you have to stop letting out to those that have no value for a good thing.

It is far better than repeating the same mistake by making your business with the same set of foolish of people that will run you down. You see, in this world, *"Majorities always forget where it actually sun-dried them after a heavy downpour, which soaked them to the marrow of their bones."*

Giving or letting is not foolishness. If they like, they should, because of that not having any word of greeting with you ever again; it doesn't really matter. Nor in anyway taking a walk by your street or area as they may choose to be in order to make you feel it so very badly; I advice you encourage yourself. Being it that they were your regular customers before and at the same time being frequent in your home due to a certain degree of intimacy, make them know that you are not in anyway short of foots in your home. Provided you have your property secured or else the landlord could turn a tenant into a beggar overnight, which is ever what the bad customers wish for you.

What Positives can Negatives Produce?

It could be good a malice, for the purpose of exercising avoidance. For example, malice can make you avert that mess, especially if those that can ruin your business are angry with you. After all, what else can negatives produce? The wishes of enemies is that those on top should fall down equal to or even below their levels. It can also help to protect your life against enemies and the danger they might harbour in their minds against you.

There are intruders; truly speaking they exist. If they haven't treated you badly, you can't know them. Human beings like you and I are teachers of bad and good lessons. But it happens that, in this world, there are some ingrates amongst your dealings who cannot appreciate any good. And instead of fighting them, when they get on your nerves, the best thing is to avoid them, in order to avert some disaster.

Therefore, in between that range and the time you will resume your formal relationship, depends on the individual, how their mind was during those crash periods before the bone of contention was over.

Now, when an incident happens, your reaction at the sport, determines your state of mind, as to whether it is going to be called malice or not. You can discover whether an individual has the atom of enmity in their inner man or not. If nothing provokes it, it doesn't function to fulfil one or two of its contents. For example, you get to know of it when you are offended. Whether or not, your state of mind, (after being hurt by neighbours, siblings or others), is malice.

Be actually sincere to yourself. If you didn't reason any bad, why the separation in the first place? It sharpens your mentality in order to pre-inform yourself, to make you wise up against any future reoccurrence of trials and temptations of similarity. He that falls twice and even continues to fall is the complete fool, okay. Take notice of friends and enemies.

Pay Attention Malice is Disguised

Malice has gone up to the level of extremism in the heart of mankind. Malice is a killer (virus/disease). In the history of man, it was reported that Cain so harboured hatred in his mind that it allowed the passion for his sibling to leave him; killing Abel his brother as a result, simply because Abel's offering was accepted by God while his own was rejected (in the Genesis of brotherhood Gen. 4:1-16).

"How could he have treacherously murdered his brother?" one asks. Simply because Abel was noted by Cain, to be originally God's, this was the reason for such hatred towards his blood brother.

Malice does one thing in the heart of man in that it can hide its killing and harming tricks until they are successfully accomplished or carried out. Just like a predator, who intelligently strategizes its prey until he succeeds. A fellow could be angry with you, yet he or she is the best to laugh with you, show you a smile and even assist you in some cases.

At least, if that is what it takes to succeed you as far as the mission is concerned, it is a done issue. The devil only learns one thing, how to cover his identity. The day he is noticed, that marks the end of his ministry of killing tricks. And so, Satan can be regarded as an author of disguise.

CHAPTER 19

Love of Hatred

Bitterness

This is an act of ill-attitude or bitterness that one develops towards another. It is a situation where sets of people deliberately just dislike you, without a cause. Is it that surprising? Well, there are so many reasons behind this. Such could be viewed in two categories or rather two dimensions. The first is spiritual while the second is physical. It could also be your fate. When they see you, they are offended. One would begin to imagine why? Their minds are so heavy with a load of hostility and grudges they cannot find opportunity to express in order to satisfy their wicked fleshly desire towards you.

They have reasons, which you might be ignorant to. Something somewhere is relating to them about your story;

which makes them stay in your life to disturb you. You could call them foundational powers, monitoring agents or even intelligent evil students with knowledge of your background from an evil school of thought, where demons are their teacher. It is either they die or the memory of your tale is totally erased off their skulls, without which they can never stop disturbing you. By the power in the name of Jesus, I rubbish every memory about you in the skull of your enemies against your life in Jesus' name.

Spiritual Traders

There are spiritual traders. Heaven is aware of this. You must believe me that if you are sold spiritually and the buyers are not given the freedom or chance to operate their mind towards you; the only thing they can do is to express their feelings with anger. It is either you have hooked them with prayers or one other thing has restricted them from hurting or harming you. That is why the scripture says: *"No weapon formed against you shall prosper."* Secondly, *"Whoever that gathers together against you shall fall for your sake."* The last but not the least, *"Do not give the devil a chance to take advantage of you, for you are no more ignorant of his devices"* (Isa. 54:15, 17; 2 Cor. 2:11).

If enemies can't secure a loophole to attack you, it means, a mission failure to them. The result of dragging property, (that belongs to you in the spiritual realm), which they could not succeed to collect, is hatred. Certain powers like: demons, evil forces, occult powers and others may want you to surrender your soul and peradventure you refuse them, that could arouse their ganging up against you all over. The simple fact is that the system of the world is organised and it is under the control and influence of demonic powers. Believe it or not, a simple layman's understanding about this issue is that it was a demon that disvirgined you (directly or indirectly). I leave it with you to check it out.

The Anger of Malice

Physically, when gossipers have spread your news around to bad people, whenever they set eyes on you they become angry. Usually, what they were related would determine their reaction towards you. They just don't care nor even want to know whether what someone has told them about you is true or false. All they care is a mission against you, that's all. The next conclusion is malice.

Someone could also have lied against you, whether to your enemies or your friends, just to isolate you. As we all know, not all friends can officially declare any lie being told to them in the secret by some other persons. Never take a pretentious personality for any friend, (for a serious friendship or a relationship) he or she could be dangerous. You can only hear anything of such where there is true likeness and such a friend is reared.

People can be recruited by far; enemies who cannot even have a direct access to you in order to help discharge their enmity on you. In the brotherhood of nature, anything can happen. In the sense, if you ask for a human part for a piece of meat he or she is ready to bring it for you; just to show to you that he cares about you, whether good or bad.

Pretentious Camouflage & Conspiracy

No chance someone will not join the other to dance. Someone can help to lie against the other (1 Kings 21:8-14). To every class of issues, there are assistances. So many persons are into a relationship, who pretended to be in love with one another. Indirectly, common love is based on conditions: in case things go on this way or that way, I will equally change this way or that way. Such a relationship is camouflage or catastrophe.

Racism is the order of their days. Believe it or not. Due to that, any little thing, offence or a mistake, he or she hates you instantly. In most cases, these sets of people always prove self-righteousness in all their doings and even claim superiority. Be wise. For human beings are ministers to many things. But the only condition here is choice. Your choice is indisputable but whatever you choose will determine as to whether your result is going to be positive or not.

If evil cannot put on a white garment to conceal many things in order to deceive with success, it means it is being stripped and a baby can even know it right away and then begin to run because no rational being stays with negativity. Evil can humbly come to you in that it can succeed in destroying you if care is not taken. But only the mercy of God can save you.

May somebody be vindicated and secured by the Lord God to His glory, in Jesus' name. Really, in the human phenomenon, one can hardly turn down anyone who comes to one in a humble manner with the intention of evil highly organised and concealed up from the inn to hurt. You can't just turn back a smile that put a partial happiness in your mind just to conceal evil harbouring behind towards you. And you as a human being lack the insight to notify the intention. May God help us.

Dangerous Pretenders

If evil can't cram or rather download any good to exhibit in order to cover its mission of havoc, it just can't succeed. If it is exposed, cataclysmic finish. And that you know must affect the ministry of evil generally. Pretension is deeply rooted in here. A most dangerous of all friends is a pretender.

Similarly, if the devil cannot laugh, can't smile, can't hug, it means he has made himself plainly known as the complete devil and that can easily kill his ministry. So, as master of negativities as being called, can disguise so as well as the followers. Whosoever is a master of any game simply knows how to play his game.

That is why you can hardly detect who is after your life without the necessary spiritual eyes. Certain humans have elements of wickedness in them in that they can do anything disgustful to you. And if you are not careful with them, you fall victim, and they harm you. May God not let enemies succeed us for their promotions in Jesus' name.

Pray for the Right People to Enter your Life

I respect the prayer, for coming in contact with the right people, (they are the real people for your life). They make things happen to you for good. You don't employ them as prayer contractors, yet they are praying for you. You did not warn them against talking bad about you, yet they just don't say anything or even a word relatively close to negative about you.

You can see however hard you may try to please people so that they can just start talking about your good, it can't really function because human beings are very hard to get along with.

Positive discussion can come from the mouths of loved and beloved ones if at all they want to discuss you, they must have one or two things to say, which remind them of your good. While on the contrary, evil communication or conversation spoil the mind of its joy and happiness; such can never sound pleasant to your hearing, trust me.

In the world of hatred, even your shape (as if one can create themselves!) can pose an offence in the heart of wicked souls, without any sign of a genuine cause. Somebody can't just simply say, *"This is the reason I hate this person."* Somebody can be aroused with offence just because you were not well grounded in education. Ask him or her, *"Do you know how much it takes to go to school, not to mention the course one might choose to study?"* Or, *"Have you ever burned the candle for one year? On what grounds where you affected that he or she did not go to school?"*

Evil Jealousy is a Witchcraft

Remember, education has no age limit. You can still do something; if it bothers you, he is not academically inclined. You can normalise the situation because it is never too late.

Stop claiming any sign of superiority over your neighbour. Please, let me take you to your level of consciousness. Remember you have none the same destiny. That has settled the number one stage. Two, you are not from the same family.

Three, you are not in the same level of human nature. Why are you so nervy about your neighbour with a reason so baseless that you will even be ashamed when analysed? I suggest you do a kind of research over your life that it could be a bewitchment of something why you are so particular about your neighbour in that perspective or manner. Evil jealousness is a witchcraft.

Take note. No single born element has any right whatsoever to pass judgment (with a speedy conclusion) when they have no real access to find out whether or not his assumptions is true. With your insinuation, you might just be wrong and even judgmental. Please, I advise you drop your sentiment. Even if our lives network with Sovereignty, (according to destinies) doesn't give you the impetus to act perversely towards your neighbour.

The fact that humans have been made governors of the earth by the Sovereign Lord, doesn't mean, even when you are not due to interfere, you dabble just to be humanistic and personal. Your wrong actions and decisions might be offensive to God sometimes.

Be Careful where you Land Yourself

Check-balance everything you tend to do, day in and day out before even doing it to the sight of man. I suppose someone does not make him or herself a horrible personality before others nor would want to even be one either. Your mouth, we all know that it is meant to talk. But don't make any contribution, when a conversation does not concern you that much.

Your legs are your natural gift of transportation by God, you must control them else they take you to wrong places. You must control your eyes, else, they put you in trouble like David against Uriah's wife Bathsheba (the Hittite - 2 Sam. 11:2-3). Feelings are sometimes birthed after a sight and that depends on what one sees, at that particular point in time. Have you ever slept with somebody's wife without seeing her first! Have you ever stolen anything that does not belong to you, without seeing it first? I put it on you as the engine carrying your body about, to be careful on how you actually carry it about; else you land yourself in an undesirable place.

Remember, (not the body, although the body is also necessary), it's the engine that makes the vehicle. You must be conscious, as any third party, between someone and his or her situations. You may be the solution to that problem in your neighbour's life, which is not directly your own case. I am not talking about the stead of His Excellency Jehovah God; you must make yourself the lord over that situation for good, to the glory of God's name. That is when you will be blessed, after all said have done. Unnecessary interference is uncalled for. God blesses you.

CHAPTER 20

Destructive Love

Evil Missionaries

There are devilish agents in the form of personalities in the whole wide world. They are specifically errand by the devil to do nothing but to destroy our lives. Delilah was specifically errand to destroy Samson who was a divinely anointed killing machine (by God Himself), against the enemies of His people Israelites; particularly the Philistines.

As Delilah rose, I wish the lustful urge in Samson never caught the attention of Delilah, Samson wouldn't have been brought to destruction and ruin to totally forfeit the divine assignment by the living God, which was about the liberalisation of the Israelites from their oppressors.

Delilah induced Samson with fate, which actually dragged him to the mound. May the good God help and deliver us from evil missionaries who come to us in the name of love with all humility, concealed up with evil. May the angel of the God of Justice shoot the evil someone conceals up in their mind against us, in Jesus' name.

I saw that Samson suffered impatience and lacked understanding. I saw Samson suffered dilemma. I saw Samson suffer the pain of consequences, which humanity put on him, when he allowed it to control his weak-point.

He was appointed a divine leader who was holding various offices as: a prophet, a judge, king or a president and a mentor and many more directly by Jehovah Himself to minister to the Israelites. And the devil in no doubt is specifically against any good leader in his or her leadership position to the glory of God (Gen. 1:28). He—the devil must fight with tooth and nail to bring any concerned body completely down to the mound if God does not intervene.

Right from heaven was where Satan was seen as a rival to any good leadership. Jehovah God Himself is the Almighty living testimony of that. Praise be God's that he—Satan was defeated (Rev. 12:11). I don't know who has been arranged on an errand to destroy you because of your destiny, may he or she receives disappointment and failure in Jesus name. And if care is not taken, you will hear his or her obituary ceremony being announced to your hearings.

Destructions have categories of witches. One, this type now is on assignment to destroy careers. For example, a good intelligent guy or girl who is so ambitious will suddenly begin to battle with sexual urge so very high on the high clan such that is beyond cope-able with her human control measure, if care is not taken.

The next thing no doubt, he or she has to start looking for whom to practice it with in order to satisfy the desire of flesh. If peradventure, along the line he or she is able to find someone and it becomes difficult to just quit and now end up with pregnancy, what will happen to the career? It is a foregone issue.

The devil is bad in the sense, he knew very well that if he allows the targeted personality to finish his or her career, he or she must be a product of himself and glory will go to God the Creator. The fact is, any well-educated fellow is already an economically productive fellow of him or herself and family (and the nation in general), the devil has this awareness.

A technical know-how is not only for himself but also for the country he or she is found. This is better instead of the nation to have to depend on importers base on technical requirement. For the able or local industries, she can carefully make do with her citizens who have come up to that level; which costs less compared to international labour.

Human Beings are Terrorists

These sets just love to be so. The purpose might be that they just want people to hear their names in order to reign for the devil and then get them promotion and praise by seeing people crying. And that gladdens the devil's heart, even gratifies him. At this process, they waste houses, property, kill and destroy companies, market, schools etc. It is only God, who still till tomorrow likes His enemies.

Humanly, if anybody tells you that he or she likes his enemies, he is a complete liar; truth is not in him. God was a number one to have an enemy: Satan all the way from heaven (Rev. 12:3, 7-12). And so, who are you to expect exemption as far as the enemy is concerned?

Be Wiser than your Enemies

I often hear people saying they don't have enemies, but that is not faith, rather a preparation to die in ignorance! If at all, because of God, it will not be that immediately. The truth is that, human beings can be so dangerous at times in that, you can't trust anybody. The day you reconcile with a rivalry is the day you enter gear two in his next target of your downfall or even your life.

So, it is left for you to decide as to whether to readjust your belt or not. He who falls twice is the fool. The best solution is to give a distance after reconciliation. Don't trust them too much as before. I pray for somebody, go, be wiser than your enemies in Jesus' name (Ps. 119:98).

The fact that you don't want to lose any relationship, does not mean, you should endanger your life. We all know by the time you intelligently follow the enemies on their tactics against you in order to minimise falling victim all the time, the little familiarity between you and the unfriendly friends, will gradually begin to fade away.

Don't mind the process. Don't worry. It will now look as if your relationship has totally ruined or damaged and that you just can't amend to blend with each other again or anymore. If it disrupt it, let it disrupt. There are still good people in the world. Pray to God, you will locate them. Even though no single element is perfect, but at least, the ones you can easily cope with their dealings and characters, should be okay by you, if I am not mistaken.

Try and forgive them so that you can move on with your life. In future, you may have something to do in common, as a distance relationship but with consciousness. May things falling apart never be your portion, I pray for you in Jesus' name. We all have a lot to tell about some dramatic loves we have had. Some of us can't even explain their case, due to doses embedded in the whole process. I mean, it is untold. They rather shed tears to fill in the gap and then move on with their lives to explain every bit of what they experienced, which could give them frustration if not checked.

God is Your Strength & Courage

Certain humans are desperately wicked. They purposely hurt you in order to make you feel so very bad. Never mind, God is your strength and even courage. Animals aren't responsible for any breaking up relationship between two or more friends; rather humans like you and I in a mission for their master— the devil. Apart from that, they can also break up any date or courtship between couples to be in the nearest future; just to make sure they don't marry to fulfil (Gen. 1:28).

Run from the word of the serpent; for it is a venom against matrimonies. Satan is still very much fighting that verse in the scripture till tomorrow, relentlessly. This is the utmost word of all the words of the living God which covers the whole wide world and every content thereof. If it takes him to stoop so very low, he does just that provided he is able to fight it.

The Enemy has a Mission

If it costs him any kind of mood, he patronises the costless boutique in order to succeed his mission, he or she does just that. Even if he has to travel round the entire globe, he doesn't mind his ticket and begins to travel round as the case may be. Is it possible he bears your father's name, he doesn't mind denying his surname even before you. He can renounce his origin for the sake of his targeted people as a missionary.

He can change school, change course, change environment even his or her date just because of one thing the devil his master has errand him or her against the victims that he doesn't want to exist; if at all, it should exist to give him a praise else, no way.

If it takes to bleach to meet up, a done issue without impulse. You could even be wearing the same colour clothes every time, doesn't mean the purpose is achieved or accomplished. You can both make each other indispensable it doesn't really matter. Use the same creams, perfumes, shoes and make-up, still doesn't matter. If you like to be sleeping on the same bed, perhaps he or she could even turn to your house cleaner, by cleaning or washing your house and clothes, even toilet, it still does not matter because a mission is a mission.

Look! Cut the same hairstyles, it's still doesn't matter. Work in the same company, even farm together, same thing still. He or she could chat with you till tomorrow even flatter you of something, my brother it still doesn't change anything. Mission is a mission. Delilah pretended to be in love with Samson, with Samson already fallen in love with her; yet she still betrayed him. Love wasn't her mission, rather a mission to destroy a divine tool from the hand of God. You can even mate to have good time together, for a fun, but a dog that must bite must bite, except by God's intervention.

Mission Accomplished

Tell all your secrets to him or her to upload (or download) to tell how much you've confided in this person, yet you are not saved. If you like, donate your intestines into his or her public treasure, it's still doesn't change anything. He or she can because of you become even a member of same church; most importantly your soul is claimed indirectly from the kingdom of God to the kingdom of darkness, that's a mission accomplished intelligently. Be careful with human beings. The devil can be stupid and foolish at times just to capture his mugs for a bait.

The devil can claim a student to you who are not even grounded a potential student enough even when he is already a professor, one must know he is particular about something. Can you see when a landlord, (driver of hummer jeep) parks and begin to trek alongside with a cyclist in the name of intimate friendship and begins to flatter and hail the less privileged.

The fact that someone holds you so very closely with high esteem doesn't mean you are the alpha and omega in his mind. Find out what he or she wants. Then you can tell by relatively guest what exactly with all conclusion he or she actually wanted from you. Behold, with all great surprises; what someone wants you for, why he or she stooped so very low that you begin to wander wow, so lovely and kind is nothing but to turn you a complete ladder with which he can climb up and down at the end.

A Human Ladder

Like you didn't know a ladder so very well, let me define it to you. A ladder is an object which could either be made with iron or wood with different steps, which are horizontally designed on different levels. The purpose is to enable man, animal or others to be able to reach a certain level it would want to reach, which could not possibly reached alone by standing on the ground.

Attention please, this is where I actually want you to learn some lessons. You can observe that, ladder is a man made lifeless object. Already, it has no saying. Whoever wants to use it, in order to be able to climb up and reach the next level. Secondly, whoever reaches up can decide whether he is to push it down or allow it to remain at the position it was placed.

You can see that ladder as a simile to be a human being here and as a beautiful or handsome personality as it is, it can only take people up but it just can't go up except external force is being applied on it. Already it is lifeless, being that it lacks the full or complete presence of God. He or she can connect people but he is not connected. He or she is an educator but he doesn't have anything up-stairs. Not even a certificate to show.

He makes couples to settle down but he is a single to the core. He knows how to plan with people in order to make a good use of their resources but can't just account for his own income. In short, he or she has nothing to write home about. He or she can mentor people to run their homes very well but his or her home is scattered and a disaster to reckon with.

You are a ladder when you tell people about eternity and they make it right with God but you got no salvation nor even going to heaven, hell awaits you. People wanted you to start doing something first to help yourself before they now actually know where to come in to aid you up but no way, all you do is to keep on calling for a help without making any effort to helping yourself first. My friend, you are a ladder.

Those who use the ladder can decide to change the colour of it to suit their taste as it pleases them, which might not be the desire of the ladder. Being placed in a particular position is a sign of stagnation and a complete dryness. Imagine, what takes people up is being barricaded. To have been made a ladder is a sign of a total relegation to the person in question. Something must be done about it. A ladder is completely a nobody by other humans.

If you are a ladder, you are completely stripped and made susceptible to dangers and harms, if care is not taken by your fellow humans. You could be stained by your unfriendly friends without minding to clean you up. They know very well that the stain would cause you a restriction as challenges in your life. He or she can decide to fold you up with a mission to reducing your degree to a level below your standard in such a size that you can actually enter your prepared cage by them. Oh what a life!

A man of renown is being reduced to a complete nobody. God help us. The world is sick with perversion and injustice. You are delayed when you are soaked by rain and as a ladder, you are looking for a solution to sun-dry yourself for a proper outing. When you are actually soaked, you will be very much cold in that you could relatively freeze up of something with no more vibrancy.

Set Fire to the Ladder

As a ladder, you looked dried with empty pockets. You are indirectly told to go and hide yourself when it comes to the issue of money. Money talks and is the human kind of voice in here. Really, you can't actually talk and identify with your equals. Humanly, money talks. As you can't come out, you look written and logged off in the human society even among your equals. You seem forgotten with no existence.

Humanly, if you aren't seen for quite sometimes, no one cares about you anymore. Your helpers can't easily locate you. Ladder is an identity of a change of personality, figure or important figure, eminence, and what have you. Ladder is a situation, which can call attention for a total deliverance. May we not being used for a fire to make the meal as ladder can be broken to make fire for anything in Jesus' name. The issue about ladder cannot be over emphasised; the only thing, be wise.

CHAPTER 21

Love of Wisdom

The Fear of the Lord

Almost everybody wants to be wise. And to be wise is very important and you can make your parents proud of you (Prov. 10:1). Foundationally, from the perspective of God's divinity, it is declared scripturally that those who fear God and reverence Him are actually enjoying wisdom as part of their blessings. It was directly put thus: as the fear of the Lord is the beginning of wisdom (Prov. 9:10).

The fear of the Lord is the condition here and wisdom is the benefit, that which makes someone victorious over trials and temptations even challenges and oppositions. Without consulting anybody, you will definitely know what to do and do it correctly and realise the right result at the right time with wisdom to the glory of God.

Wisdom can save you from danger. When wisdom is in charge, you don't doubt your doings. People with great wisdom are always calculative in action before even they act or voice out their feelings . An intelligent person doesn't talk anyhow. An intelligent person doesn't act or rather react anyhow. He or she always considers rash and apology first before anything.

If you don't want to be rash, juxtapose before even you carry out your decision in action. If you don't want to apologise to anybody then don't act perversely else you might just find yourself condescending to apologising even to a small boy that you are old enough to be his or her parent if you reason or think of your personality even an important figure in our society.

Dignified to the Core

If you don't want any embarrassment, don't act foolishly. Whatever a man calls himself that is exactly how he or she will definitely be. If you therefore respect yourself you will be dignified even to the core.

In decision, wisdom usually juxtapose it's decision or action as to knowing whether it will favour her or not. Without impulse, wisdom can never act. Before you react, you judge yourself first if you are right or wrong else, you are guilty, is a policy of wisdom. Wisdom hardly falls rashly into whatever she does. Wisdom and understanding of God can never allow you to offend anybody rather enable you to put your dealings and actions in a quiet check and balance for peace to reign (Prov. 2:11). As wisdom commands respect, people do therefore dignify— respect those with it.

Public figure is not only by the amount of money and material wealth you have acquired to yourself; the level of wisdom you have also counts too. The wise people are counted among social elements of the global society. They are mostly found as special advisers. Wisdom counts that was why king Solomon was always located by queens and kings from far and near at his time just to listen to his words of wisdom (1 Kings 4:34). They often do things accordingly; hence, disciplinarians.

Wisdom

Wisdom doesn't determine the level of knowledge acquisition one has acquired from institutions or schools of taught rather goes beyond that. It is indeed quite a precious gift only God can give: I mean the good wisdom. It is natural. Special advisers to the government, kings, and other royal leaders, pop-starts and super stars, musical artists, etc. are people who are deeply rooted in the true wisdom of God.

They are also very careful as not to mistakenly help the devil to gain ground by having a voice through them. This is to inform you that devil is looking for that single opportunity to paste his antenna in your life for his advantage.

There are many types of wisdom. The following could be some of them: the wisdom of God, natural, technical, and wisdom of relationship, business wisdom, in keeping discretion, in respecting others. The opposite of wisdom is: cheating, deceit, tricking, whose master is Satan. Naturally, the Lord God endowed a very few number of personalities with the gift of wisdom from His divinity.

Wisdom was what developed some countries of the world. Therefore, whatever has been artificially produced by mankind for his or her consumption, is the result of wisdom. Business oriented personalities did not just wakeup one day and begin to know what to do without the assistance of wisdom of business acumen over responsibilities in the prospect.

Wisdom Avoids Mistakes

In relationship, people also apply wisdom in order to avoid mistakes or being victimised. While on the contrary others apply a devilish kind of wisdom to be able to cheat on their partners. Some bad business partners mostly cheat or deceive others just to be able to gain their selfish interest as advantages for personal enrichment at the expense of their so called partners in the business.

In the real sense, who would think that his or her business partner would let his mind be soiled as far as cheating on his fellow business personality they bargained on transacting a business together is concerned? It is either he or she accepted wrong advice or allurement against his partner in the business.

Wisdom Never Accepts Defeat

A very many are matured in learning to keep secretes while others do not know due to immaturity on how to keep it at all. And so, there is little or possibility for the enemy to set in the business and ruin it if possible. There is an adage that says, *"The wise people always dignify those that are worth it."* It is not that they are cowards, it just that they simply know how to make good use of what they have and also to express the feeling that they value the quality of a good thing.

Wisdom is a ministry of its own. It can always give you a hope to looking forward for your future life. Wisdom can never accept defeat so easily.

Instead, it must think back as to knowing why she failed in her first attempt in order to pick correction for the next launching for a victory. The number of times wisdom failed does not really count rather what matters most is how she is able to correct her errors and rise to victory by quickly pick up from the angle or point of a concluded failure. It is a propelling force of the confidence and belief we have from God. With the help of wisdom, one can easily obey God.

A Clear Conscience Fears no Accusation

Wisdom makes you speak the truth always and that makes you become very bold because a clean conscience fears no accusation. The wise change people around them for good. This is because whenever any fellow is acting perversely around them, they straighten and correct him or her of the mistake and error immediately.

We also have the wisdom of Satan who rigorously steals knowledge and wisdom, trying to claim it as his own. Wisdom is power as well as knowledge. The originality in the wisdom of God never fades, which sustains it irrespective of the challenges and battles it faces.

At first approach, wisdom could look fake and nothing before a lay man but at the long run, it is highly appraised, even embraced. Be informed that wisdom induces the concerned with understanding and enables them to go far. Enlightenments originate from the ocean of wisdom and understanding.

To conclude this book (1 of 5), in this series called, "Love Distinguished," we close on the love of wisdom.

Ministry Profile

Doctor Agene Justice Onotiemoria (A.J.O.) hails from Uwessan Ibhiolulu, Irrua Essan Central Local Government of Edo State Nigeria. He had his primary education in Uwessan Ibhiolulu, Irrua, his post primary education in Ujabhole Grammar School, Ujabhole, Irrua and Agba Grammar School, Uromi, all in Edo State. A degree holder in Theology from LifeStyle International Christian University, Firenze Italy.

The author is humility personified, kind hearted, soft spoken and cool-headed gentleman to the core. A seasoned writer, a preacher and a pioneer of righteousness. An ordained worker of God's Vineyard as a financial secretary, an usher, a gospel musician, a member of the choir, youth speaker and a deacon. He was formerly a distributor to G.N.L.D. (an Italian company), a civil servant to Bendel Construction Company Limited (B.C.C.L.) Nigeria, and a furniture maker. He is married with a wife and children.

To Contact the Author

Please email:

Agene Justice Onotiemoria
Email: littlejustice508@gmail.com

Please include your prayer requests and comments when you write.

Other Books

The Wonderland of Love
(Love Distinguished - Series Two)

This book is the second book in this series; the title being "The Wonderland of Love." I love this concept, as love has many dimensions, covering such topics as Fake and Genuine Love, also in regards to boyfriend, girlfriend, husband, wife and children. The list is endless but a great read.

ISBN: 978-1-909132-30-6, Pages: 235,
Format: Paperback, Published: 2018
**Also available in eBook format!*

The Heart of Love
(Love Distinguished - Series Three)

The Heart of Love has to be received by the Love of Truth; it is a positive foundational footing for any house that wishes to stand. It is also known as justice that builds a nation. The bible says: The righteous are as bold as lions (Proverbs 28:1).

ISBN: 978-1-909132-31-3, Pages: 255,
Format: Paperback, Published: 2023
**Also available in eBook format!*

Sweet Bitter Love
(Love Distinguished - Series Four)

Dr. Justice again has put together stimulating truth, saying that you cannot see someone and quickly conclude that they are your bosom friends. In other words, don't be too fast to put your trust or love in those that might turn out to be bitter or sweet.

ISBN: 978-1-909132-83-2, Pages: 246,
Format: Paperback, Published: 2023
**Also available in eBook format!*

Stolen Love
(Love Distinguished - Series Five)

In this last book of this series, the writer declares that whoever one may be, whatever they do, no matter their race, background, education, class, height, structure, beauty, handsome, rich, poor, barren, married or single or otherwise, they must not allow true love to be distorted or stolen. Remember, all must stand before Him.

ISBN: 978-1-909132-84-9, Pages: 237,
Format: Paperback, Published: 2023
**Also available in eBook format!*

All Books Available

at

APMI PUBLICATIONS

Email: publications@alanpateman.com
Also Available from Amazon.com
and other retail outlets.

www.ingramcontent.com/pod-product-compliance
Lightning Source LLC
LaVergne TN
LVHW010055110826
845155LV00028B/353

* 9 7 8 1 9 0 9 1 3 2 2 8 3 *